C0-BGF-416

THE UNITED KINGDOM

The United Kingdom

A SURVEY OF BRITISH INSTITUTIONS TO-DAY

T. K. DERRY, D.Phil.

NEW YORK UNIVERSITY PRESS   1963

Library of Congress Catalog Card Number: 63-12058
© T. K. Derry, 1961

First published in Great Britain, by Longmans,
Green & Co., Ltd.
Manufactured in the United States of America

342.42
D448u

Mal. Govt.
Dec. 5, 1963

PREFACE

THE institutions of the United Kingdom have changed so rapidly in recent years that a new survey may be found useful by the general reader as well as by the student. In the belief that conciseness will be a recommendation in the eyes of those many people who are chiefly interested in the overall picture and the general trends at the present day, the historical material has been restricted to what is still needed to show how existing rules and practices first took shape. The main object of the book is to describe as faithfully as possible the framework of our national and local self-government, but particular attention has been paid to the growth of the welfare state, the changes in the role of the monarchy, and the altered status of the United Kingdom in relation to the former British territories overseas.

Students will find here all they need for an outline course on the British constitution. Those proceeding to more advanced syllabuses are referred to the reading list at the end of the book, which in conjunction with the chronological table and supplementary notes should enable them to make this introductory manual a satisfactory basis for further work.

CONTENTS

PREFACE   v

I. INTRODUCTORY   1
1. The Welfare State
2. British Conservatism
3. British Freedom
4. The United Kingdom

II. THE VOTER AND HIS VOTE   16
1. History of the Franchise
2. The Machinery of Election
3. The Function of Party
4. The Member and His Constituency

III. THE HOUSES OF PARLIAMENT   29
1. Historical
2. Control of the Public Purse
3. Legislation
4. The Parliamentary Day

IV. THE CABINET   49
1. Privy Council and Cabinet
2. The Work of a Cabinet Minister
3. The Prime Minister
4. Her Majesty's Opposition

Contents

V. THE MONARCHY — 64
1. The Basis of Law and Tradition
2. The Powers of the Queen
3. The Queen and the Commonwealth
4. Powers of the Crown

VI. THE QUEEN'S COURTS — 84
1. Their Evolution
2. The Courts of Law To-day
3. The Law and the Citizen

VII. THE SERVICE OF THE CROWN — 100
1. The Armed Forces
2. The Civil Service
3. Paying For It

VIII. SOME CENTRAL SERVICES — 116
1. Social Insurance and Social Assistance
2. The National Health Service
3. The Scientific Civil Service
4. Nationalized Industries

IX. LOCAL GOVERNMENT — 131
1. Historical
2. The Local Councils of To-day
3. How Local Councils Do Their Work

X. LOCAL GOVERNMENT SERVICES — 144
1. A Matter of Finance
2. Education
3. Housing

Contents

XI. THE GOVERNMENT OF LONDON 157
   1. Elective Authorities
   2. Other Metropolitan Institutions

XII. THE PUBLIC WORK OF WOMEN 165
   1. Historical
   2. Some Achievements

XIII. SOCIETIES WITHIN THE STATE 172
   1. The Churches
   2. Trade Unions
   3. Organizations for Social Service

XIV. THE COMMONWEALTH 184
   1. Imperial Revolution
   2. Relations between the United Kingdom and Other Member States
   3. The Dependencies

XV. BRITAIN AND INTERNATIONAL INSTITUTIONS 204
   1. Before the Second World War
   2. The New Europe
   3. World Organization

   Dates of Statutes and Other Main Events 221
   Notes and Definitions 224
   Books for Further Study 233
   Index 237

I

INTRODUCTORY

1. THE WELFARE STATE

A CENTURY ago, in the heyday of Victorianism, Walter Bagehot wrote a book on *The English Constitution*, which first introduced this kind of study to the attention of the general public. Bagehot's book is still a classic of the subject, but to turn its pages to-day is to be reminded of the important fact that the continuity of British institutions, which we rightly cherish, has not been allowed to prevent —though it may tend to obscure from unreflecting minds —revolutionary changes of emphasis and purpose. The very phrase 'welfare state', so commonly used to describe our modern society, would have conveyed no meaning to Bagehot. Had it been explained to him, as editor of *The Economist* he would have found the whole idea repugnant, and his readers would have agreed with him that welfare was the business of the individual, to which the state made its proper contribution by narrowly circumscribing its own business and its consequent expenditure.

It was both a cause and to some extent also an effect of this severe restriction of state activities that the politically active public, to which Bagehot addressed his book, was then but a small fraction of the whole. Politics was the preserve of a very limited governing class, influenced at election times—and more haphazardly on other occasions of popular excitement—by the enfranchised middle class and by pressure groups enjoying some support from the unenfranchised masses. But the issues of the day usually had no obvious connection, for better or worse, with the hard-earned living of the poor. Nor did the character of those representatives of the state who were most in evidence encourage the idea that it might be made the instrument of public welfare: the police constable, the workhouse master, the collector of rates and taxes, and (after 1870) the school attendance officer each represented an unwelcome regime imposed from above. This was a situation which changed only gradually, even after the parliamentary franchise was enlarged by the acts of 1867 and 1884: we may perhaps date from the moment when the old age pensioners drew their first weekly five shillings under the law of 1908 the mass realization that British institutions might be adapted to give positive help to the masses.

The term 'welfare state' is said to be of German origin, as was certainly the telling description of its predecessor as the 'night-watchman state'. It is also true that Bismarck's insurance laws of the 1880s marked the effective beginning of the great change. Nevertheless, it is in postwar Britain that the movement has established itself most firmly among the major powers of the western world. The most casual visitor from abroad is aware of the generous provisions of the health service; the colonial immigrant contrasts the public assistance arrangements of the United Kingdom with something far more meagre at home. As for the native, the beneficent activities of the state accompany him from the cradle to the grave—from the pre-natal clinic to the grant-aided burial. At every stage the newly created institutions of the modern state provide for the individual an increasingly high national minimum standard. He may improve upon this by his own efforts if he so chooses, but the weight of the taxation needed to maintain what the state provides makes it increasingly difficult to reach beyond it—for example, in private schools and private medical practice. Thus the sphere of state action tends to grow, and the equalizing effects of high taxes to become more and more marked.

In time of war the impact of the state and its institutions, such as military service, was always great. What is new is a pervasive state influence on the peaceful avocations of civilian life, which causes the rising generation to see the state less as an austere guardian and more as a rather possessive kind of nurse. In such circumstances changes are more frequent than in earlier days, and on the whole of greater general interest. Moreover, it makes a fascinating study to try to see how, in Britain, so much that is very new has been successfully built into an ancient traditional framework.

2. BRITISH CONSERVATISM

When foreign journalists describe the British way of life as intensely conservative, which they still do, they are certainly not thinking of the successes of a particular political party. The swing of the pendulum operates so effectively, as regards the change of electoral opinion over long periods, that since 1832 a government of Conservative complexion in the party sense has in fact held office for almost exactly half the time. But British institutions are continuously affected by a national habit of mind, which we must agree to call conservative or at least preservative, there being few countries in the modern world where links with the past, however rusty, are so jealously preserved. Some parts of our constitutional apparatus have survived from the days of the Anglo-Saxon Heptarchy to adorn the present Commonwealth system; and on the occasion of our latest revolution, nearly three centuries ago, the transfer of the crown to William and Mary was justified on the express ground that James II, the sovereign whom they ousted, had 'subverted the *ancient* rights and liberties of the people of this Kingdom'. Contrast with this the history of the USSR, which in the course of two generations has sought to make all things new; of Germany, where the old can remember four wholly different regimes; of France, with the tremendous break at 1789; and of the United States of America, whose Declaration of Independence in 1776 announced to the world the arguments on which the deliberately planned breach of continuity was to be based.

The British belief in the virtue of an unbroken history is brought home to us by occasions of ceremonial pageantry, much of which would be swept away as being insufferably cumbersome, wasteful, and even ludicrous, if it did not serve to link the present with the past. The accession of a new sovereign, for instance, is nowadays a simple and uncontested matter of fact. Yet it involves the assembling at St. James's Palace of privy councillors and 'numbers of other principal gentlemen of quality'—a body closely resembling the Witenagemot which nominated the Anglo-Saxon kings—followed by a meeting of the privy council (the Tudor organ of government), at which the sovereign among other things swears to maintain the church of Scotland (required by a Scottish statute of 1704); and finally there is the actual proclamation by a college of heralds, which was incorporated by the last ruler of mediaeval England. As for the long and intricate observances of the coronation itself, the experiment of televising them in 1953 proved an amazing success. The success was not merely that of a superbly produced show. The millions of Queen Elizabeth II's subjects, who were enabled in some measure to join in the traditional solemnities, were for a moment linked in spirit with the crowd which, following much the same coronation order, once thronged the precincts of the abbey church of Westminster to acclaim Harold Godwinsson and William of Normandy.

A coronation occurs only once in a generation, on an average, but other pageants, of a more everyday character, are equally instructive. For all Londoners the most obvious is the state opening of parliament, though the significant part is not the crowded scene as the royal coach passes between the palace and Westminster, but the hushed spectacle inside the house of lords. The queen takes her place upon the throne of the realm, with her consort, the great officers of state, and the judges in attendance; the lords spiritual and temporal sit in order of precedence upon the red benches before her: only the commons, with the Speaker and the prime minister at their head, stand humbly at the bar of the house. Thus is reproduced the original *parliamentum* of magnates and officials, to which Edward I and his successors summoned representatives of shire and borough to give their consent and perhaps voice their grievances—but not to confer as equals. The Queen reads 'her' Speech, in which her ministers have carefully outlined their proposals for the new session and for the needs of a democratic state—the formalities have bridged six centuries.

The provinces have no show to compare with this, but the minor ceremonies with which the sheriff is legally obliged to receive the judges at assizes connect us with an even remoter past. For when judges first rode their circuits in the twelfth century, the sheriffs who received them as the king's representatives, shire by shire, had already ruled their shires for a matter of two or three hundred years. Nor does the office of mayor in a typical English borough lack elements of pageantry—the chain of office and the mace-bearers—which recall Latin charters, given perhaps by a Plantagenet.

The continuity of our institutions is a thing of which we may well be proud, but the conservative spirit which retains old ceremonies depends upon something more than antiquarian enthusiasm. It depends upon a formal respect for law, which preserves what has once been duly prescribed. It depends also upon our knowledge that such ceremonies, by their common appeal, bind us together man to man, as well as binding each new generation to those that went before. Finally, it depends upon a principle of reverence. In a democratic age the Englishman still welcomes something he can look up to: an ancient symbolic proceeding fulfils this role for him inasmuch as it bears witness to a glorious past.

3. BRITISH FREEDOM

Freedom, even more than conservatism, is characteristic of the institutions which our forefathers struggled to establish. This was true over two centuries ago, when Hogarth drew his famous 'Calais Gate' to point a contrast between the free-born Englishman and the downtrodden foreigner. At one time, indeed, much ceremonial of the type that we have been discussing, from the state opening of parliament to the kissing of hands by ministers, derived a heightened interest from the fact that half the world sought to imitate our august form of government. Parliaments which owed a debt to Westminster (acknowledged or unacknowledged) were among the first-fruits of five great revolutions—the American, the French, the South American, the Belgian, and the Italian—all occurring within a hundred years, and after 1870 some approximation to our cabinet system began to establish itself in almost every European state.

To-day the position is different. Nazism and Fascism, which dominated political thinking in the decade before the war of 1939, have indeed been swept away; but this does not necessarily mean a general return to government by cabinets dependent upon any genuinely democratic parliamentary system. In Soviet Russia and China the world sees a pattern of state, immensely strong and commanding the absolute loyalty of its subjects, which has evolved out of the communist revolution into political forms and by political methods which, though employing the phrases of democracy, have little in common with its realities as we understand them. In eastern and central Europe and elsewhere, other states emerging from the chaos of war, victors and vanquished alike, have found themselves powerfully attracted by the success of the great Russian experiment, or are at best uncertain whether democracy in the British sense of the word is compatible with the need for quick and resolute decisions in a troubled world. Even within the Commonwealth there are member states which have failed to maintain the freedoms of British political practice in times of stress.

It is not, be it noted, the reality of this freedom which is denied, but its value. Indeed, a French writer who was

Hogarth's contemporary already saw that freedom was not the only possible *raison d'être* of the state.

> The monarchies with which we are familiar have not, like those of which we have just been talking [i.e. England], liberty as their direct object: they aim only at the glorificaton of the citizens, the State, the prince.[1]

If we substitute 'prestige' for 'glory', this would be a very fair description of the motive that lies behind many of the activities of Nazism and Fascism in more recent times. The glorification motive may have perished finally with Hitler and Mussolini and their Japanese counterparts; but the world which they so nearly conquered still finds liberty a weaker motive than the pursuit of national security. There is also an economic motive to be reckoned with. The state whose aim is the liberty of the citizen has too often provided chiefly the liberty to starve, whereas the new kind of state, which deploys the whole of the national resources, including the labour of all its citizens, does in return guarantee work and wages for all. In so far as the guarantee is honestly operated, it has obvious advantages over any system of unemployment assistance. But to determine how often the result is more nearly akin to a form of state slavery would lead us too far from our subject. Instead, let us see just what the foreigner means when, perhaps with a shrug of the shoulders, he contrasts our country with his as above all 'a free country'.

To the ordinary man under any government the state means chiefly a network of laws and regulations which he has to obey. Under the conditions of modern life these are always increasing, for example, the regulations in the

[1] Montesquieu: *L'Esprit des Lois* (1748), XI, 7.

highway code. In matters of that kind rules are as numerous and stringent in Britain as in any other country: where, we may ask, is the evidence of freedom? The answer lies in the Rule of Law, a name given to one of the principles that lie at the very root of our constitutional system. In Britain there is no such thing as arbitrary power—every action by which the government governs the subject must be authorized by law, either by statute law passed by parliament or by the ancient principles of common law, which have been recognized for many hundreds of years. The test is that all government actions can be appealed against in the ordinary law courts, where judges, over whom the government has no influence, will decide whether or not they are thus authorized. This remains the general rule, though in recent years there have been encroachments upon it which have excited some alarm: these we shall refer to later.

Generally speaking, then, the British citizen is free to do as he likes, so long as he does not break any definite law, and when he is accused of such a breach, must be presumed innocent until he is proved to be guilty. But our freedom also depends upon certain less easily defined traditions of liberty. Three of these may be specified because they run directly counter to the ideas which are fostered by some other forms of government. One is our inherent distrust of officials and officialdom: there is probably no civilized country where the official as such receives so little respect as in Britain, and certainly no place where such a jealous eye is kept upon the limits of his powers. Consider, for instance, the indignation which is so quickly aroused in parliament when an over-zealous police officer arrests some palpably innocent person by mistake. A second tradition, on which (as we shall see) the effective working of our parliamentary system depends, is our national habit of tolerating the opinions of a minority with which we happen to disagree. This habit, measured by an absolute standard, may have lost some of its force in recent years—but not by comparison with the intolerance of our continental neighbours, confronted as they often are by circumstances of greater stress.

A third closely related tradition is that which defends the right to the free expression of opinion. The laws against slanderous speech and libellous publications are just as strict as in other countries, and in some respects stricter; and there are statutes, some of them dating from the Napoleonic wars, which would legally entitle the police to ban almost any vigorous open-air demonstration. But the public expectation has long been quite otherwise. The signed letter to *The Times* and the political pamphlet sold in large numbers over the imprint of a flourishing left-wing publisher; the provocative argument on television and the provocative slogan carried on a banner to a meeting in Hyde Park—these, no less than the free expression of views between individuals, can be interfered with by authority only at the risk of outraging a most formidable body of opinion. The Radical agitators of the past have left no party behind them, but their ideas have permeated the mind of the nation.

But behind all this there remains the fact that the British are a free people primarily because they are a self-governing people. As the main object of this book is to try to explain how this self-government works, we need not stress the point now. But it is important to remember that the British parliament, freely elected by the people, itself has freedom to do anything. The parliaments of many other countries, such as the United States congress, have only restricted powers: there are certain constitutional laws, or certain treaties among the different peoples out of which the state is formed, that parliament is powerless to alter. But our parliament can alter the succession to the throne or reverse the whole economic system of the country by the same processes and in the same space of time as it takes to extend the school-leaving age or alter the duty on tea. So far from constitutional laws being sacrosanct in Britain, there is not even any agreement as to which laws are 'constitutional'—a marked contrast with America, where the constitution with its amendments is printed as a familiar 20-page document. Thus our constitution may fairly be described as 'flexible': it can be adapted to meet new needs with the absolute minimum of fuss and delay.

This is all-important because it is the people who decide what parliament shall or shall not do. Therefore the sovereignty of parliament and its omnicompetence imply that the people represented by parliament in the last analysis enjoy a sovereign freedom.

4. THE UNITED KINGDOM

The 'people represented by parliament' is a designation that has been subject to several changes in the course of the political development of the British Isles. To begin with they were only the English, until a Welshman's grandson, Henry VIII, added 23 members of parliament for Wales (and four for Monmouthshire). The representatives of Scotland, 16 lords and 45 commons, were included in the parliament at Westminster by the act of union in 1707, when the monarchy of 'Great Britain'—the style first adopted by James VI and I in a proclamation of

October 1604—became the monarchy of the 'United Kingdom'. From 1801 to 1920 the ambit of parliament reached its fullest extent with the inclusion of the people of Ireland, of whom only one-third are left within the limits of the main successor state, the United Kingdom of Great Britain and Northern Ireland. Commonly referred to as 'the United Kingdom', this book will treat it for the most part as a single whole. But mention may first be made of some important institutional differences still to be found within the kingdom and the small neighbouring possessions of the crown.

By the treaty of 1707 Scotland made two specific reservations. One was for the safety of the presbyterian church of Scotland, which is still the established, privileged church in North Britain, and of which the queen becomes a member whenever she crosses the Border. The other was for the distinctive Scottish judicial system, which since the sixteenth century had been based partly on the reception of Roman law. Laws enacted since 1707 apply to both countries, but common law (including land law and the law of marriage) and methods of procedure in Scotland are entirely different. Juries can return a majority verdict and are allowed to decide that the case is 'not proven'; the first two judges are styled lord president and lord justice clerk; and the highest Scottish court is the court of session at Edinburgh, from which, however, a further appeal in civil cases lies to the house of lords. Two other institutions, not mentioned in the treaty, were left untouched at the time. In local government provost, bailie, and large burgh are terms roughly corresponding to mayor, alderman, and non-county borough; the four largest cities have the same status as English county boroughs; but the Scottish counties, being less populous, delegate fewer powers to district councils, and the distribution of functions is in other respects still somewhat different. As regards education, Scotland in 1707 already had (or seriously strove for) a school in every parish, with four universities for a population of one million; and until the education act of 1944 is fully carried out she remains still ahead of England both in the general respect paid to education and in some of the actual facilities. It is this tradition which most clearly distinguishes the Scotsman to-day. With the modern increase in the functions of government Scotland has received another mark of separateness, in the creation of a Scottish Office, the head of which has been since 1926 a full secretary of state. This department deals separately with Scottish agriculture, education, health (including housing), and Home Office business. There is also a Scottish Committee in the house of commons, consisting mainly of the M.P.s for Scotland, to which all Scottish bills are referred for consideration.

There is no separate Department for Wales: the principality was originally conquered territory, and its institutions have been thoroughly assimilated to those of England. The Welsh, however, have their own living language, to which the annual eisteddfod or 'session of the bards' bears vigorous witness; and this is recognized, notably in the maintenance of a Welsh subdivision of the ministry of education, with its own inspectorate and advisory council. The Welsh M.P.s also at one time formed a separate group at Westminster, which scored an important victory for the spirit of Welsh nationalism in 1920, when the church of England, which had been the established church of Wales for more than three centuries, finally lost its privileges and was put on a footing of equality with the native nonconformist organizations. A more recent concession has been the appointment of a minister for Welsh affairs, who combines some other post in the cabinet with the control of a small body of civil servants in Cardiff to deal with the special needs of the principality.

In Ireland there has occurred, since the First World War, an almost complete break with the history of the four preceding centuries, emphasized by the division of the island into two separate antagonistic parts, the larger of which became first a dominion and finally an independent republic outside the Commonwealth (see p. 195). But the six counties of Northern Ireland—two-thirds of the ancient province of Ulster—are a land long settled by Scots and English, considerably industrialized and having a protestant majority among its one and a quarter million inhabitants. Since 1920 its form of government has been dual. The British connection, to which the typical Ulsterman is intensely loyal, is emphasized by the retention of a dozen members of parliament and by submission to Westminster in all matters of foreign policy and military arrangements; the British government also collects the taxes, returning the balance left after payment for the 'reserved services'. For local affairs, on the other hand, Northern Ireland has its own parliament, consisting of a house of commons of 52 elected members and a smaller senate elected mainly by the lower house. The titular head is a governor, appointed by the queen, who rules through a cabinet, so that the system as a whole constitutes a kind of half-way house between the status of a part of the United Kingdom and that of a separate member state of the Commonwealth.

It remains to notice, by way of contrast, two lesser insular appendages of Britain, neither of which ever suffered that representation in the parliament of the United

Kingdom, from which southern Ireland has freed itself. The Channel Islanders boast that they conquered England, not vice versa, by which dark saying they allude to the fact that their islands are earlier possessions of that duchy of Normandy from which the Conqueror sailed. Like Wales, they have their own language (a kind of French patois); like Scotland, they have their own customary law and law courts; and in addition there survive for parliaments the ancient estates of Jersey and Guernsey. The Isle of Man has similar picturesque survivals, though there the legislative body, the Tynwald, is of Norse origin. But if the Channel Isles are the earliest, Man is among the latest acquisitions of the British crown, since the lordship of Man remained until the eighteenth century in the hereditary possession of the earls of Derby, successors to the kings of the sagas. Our acts of parliament, though not our income tax, are commonly adopted by the islanders, both of the English Channel and of the Irish Sea; a lieutenant-governor is appointed by the crown; and joint affairs fall, like so many oddments of business, within the province of the home secretary.

II

THE VOTER AND HIS VOTE

1. HISTORY OF THE FRANCHISE

WE saw in the last chapter that Britain is a free country inasmuch as every citizen shares in the control of the government by means of the vote, which goes to choose a member of parliament for his or her neighbourhood. This right to vote, or franchise, was not always the possession of every citizen. Indeed, down to 1832, when the modern history of the franchise may be said to begin, the vote in rural England was restricted entirely to landowners, while in those towns which returned M.P.s—the parliamentary boroughs—there were all kinds of different systems of voting, the majority of which reserved the privilege for a few special inhabitants, such as the mayor and corporation. The justification for this system was that it gave representation to the land (that is to say, to agriculture, then the most important national interest) and to the different classes (because the variety of franchise in the boroughs meant that every class, even the poorest, predominated somewhere).

Since 1832, however, the franchise has been based on the idea of representing individuals rather than the ancient 'commons (communities) of the realm'. That is why the limit fixed by the great reform act in that year lasted such a short time. The vote had been given to the middle class

—ten-pound householders in the boroughs and substantial tenant-farmers in the country districts: why should a house that cost £10 a year or a farm of £50 (or less if the lease was for a long term of years) confer the franchise and a £9 house or a £49 farm confer nothing? Hence the acts of 1867 and 1884, the former of which gave the vote to all householders in boroughs, irrespective of the value of their houses, and to lodgers in boroughs, provided that their lodgings cost them £10 a year unfurnished. The latter conferred precisely the same franchises upon householders and lodgers in country districts. Thus by 1884 England—and, indeed, the whole United Kingdom of Great Britain and Ireland, to every part of which these measures finally applied—had what passed for a democratic system. But it is important to notice that the poorer lodgers, sons residing in their parents' houses, the many people who did not remain in one place for the twelve months required to get their names placed on the official register of voters, and all persons in receipt of poor relief still had no power to vote.

On the eve of the first world war, the franchise was possessed by 37 per cent of the total male population: that is to say, about one-third of the men as well as all the women of full age were still without the vote. Changes since then have been rapid. The Representation of the People Act of 1918 made six months' residence the sole necessary qualification for a man to exercise the franchise —manhood suffrage at last—and included women above the age of 30 on practically the same terms as men. Ten years later the age limit for women was reduced to 21 and universal suffrage established—except for minors, peers of the realm, persons of unsound mind, prisoners serving sentences of more than 12 months for treason or felony, and anyone found guilty of electoral corruption within the preceding seven years. At the same time a privilege of wealth, whereby the same person could have several votes for residences and business premises in different constituencies, was reduced by limiting an election to one day and allowing a maximum of two votes, which had to be for different classes of qualification. In 1946 this plural voting was completely abolished.

A second type of parliamentary reform was that which aimed at making the votes cast equally effective by a fairer distribution of seats. Before 1832 there had been a strict separation between county seats, of which each English county had two but those of Wales and Scotland only one, and the far more numerous pairs of borough seats. The bulk of these were attached to ancient towns in the south of England, many of which were ludicrously small in comparison with the new industrial centres of the north. The Great Reform Act of 1832 therefore deprived the smaller boroughs of one or both of their seats, and these were given to the rising towns and to the more populous counties. But for another fifty years there remained some traces of the old system—it was a greater honour to represent a county as 'knight of the shire' than to represent a borough, however large; and many ancient boroughs retained two members although their population was very much smaller than that of a new town with only one. This was remedied by the redistribution act of 1885, which abolished all these ancient survivals and divided the whole country into constituencies of roughly equal population. The big towns were carved up into districts, each returning one member, the counties into divisions, likewise returning one member each. The only exception was those boroughs which had always returned two members and happened to have the population which entitled them still to return two: in those places, as in the middle ages, each voter still had a double vote.

The redistribution of seats must obviously be continued from time to time, as the tide of population in particular areas rises and falls. Since 1945 parliament has taken the more drastic step of subdividing the most populous constituencies, so as to raise the total number of seats from 625 to 640, later reduced again to 630. In the interests of uniformity the remaining double-member constituencies have also been divided. Finally, the abolition of plural voting (already referred to) brought to an end the separate representation of universities. There had been M.P.s for Oxford and Cambridge since the reign of James I, but as the privilege had been extended to newer universities and the franchise was made equally available to all graduates, the ballot-papers being distributed by post, it was a privilege of intellect rather than wealth. Its abolition deprived parliament of a small group of independent minds, which has left a gap.

2. THE MACHINERY OF ELECTION

Having seen how the election, from being the direct concern of a small minority, has become the business to a strictly equal degree of the whole nation, we may now consider what actually happens at an election. The scene is familiar enough to most of us, but we may perhaps recall it in the words of a writer who looks back with regret to the old days, when candidates, voters, and rival mobs confronted each other in public, first at the hustings, where the candidates made open-air speeches on being nominated, and then at the polling-booth, where (until 1872) votes were publicly recorded. He contrasts the present thus:

> The polling lasts only one day and in the great town it is usually a quiet and dull day. The town hall, or an elementary school, or some other public building, has replaced the polling-booth. In the middle of the large bare room the row of sentry-boxes of rough boarding is erected. At an unimpressive table sit the returning officer and his clerks with the tin ballot-boxes in front of them.
>
> The elector strolls into the room, gives his name and address to one of the officials, receives a numbered slip of paper with the names of the candidates, takes it to one of the deal shanties to affix his cross, comes back with it folded, drops it through a slit in the tin box, and goes out. That is all: and to the voter it sometimes seems too little.[1]

The atmosphere of an election is not always so unexciting, especially where rival candidates run each other close and local feeling is involved; but tameness is the natural result of the great efforts that are made to eliminate corruption and undue influence upon the elector, though a party remains free to spend as much money as it likes upon its national appeal as distinct from what is spent inside a particular constituency. There the law keeps a jealous watch on the candidate's behaviour during the period before election day, requiring him to appoint an agent to pay all his bills and to prove, when the election is over, that the candidate's total expenditure has not exceeded a modest sum fixed by parliament. In 1948 this was reduced to £450 plus 2d. or 1½d. for each elector, the larger of the two allowances being for the more difficult canvass in a rural area. By this means the wealthy candidate is effectively prevented from corrupting the voters by gifts at

[1] Sir Sidney Low: *Governance of England*, p. 215.

election time, though it is less easy to prevent wealthy supporters from strengthening his chances by lavish expenditure for the public benefit, which may redound to the credit of the candidate they are known to favour. On the whole the secrecy of the ballot operates to prevent either a policy of expenditure or (much rarer) of intimidation on behalf of a candidate from having any decisive effect on the issue. But if there is any serious doubt about the honesty of the proceedings an election petition can be brought before a judge, who has power to find out which way individuals voted by examining the counterfoils of the numbered voting slips, which record the individual voter to whom the slip was issued; he can annul the election and inflict penalties for corruption. Such action is rarely called for, and very rarely taken.

The election period may be said to begin with the publication of the notice that the existing parliament is about to be dissolved. Under the parliament act of 1911 this must happen once every five years, but it may happen whenever the sovereign, who will normally be acting in accordance with the advice of the prime minister, is pleased to order a dissolution. A writ is then sent from the Crown Office in London, ordering the returning officer, who is the sheriff of the county or the mayor of the borough, to return a member or members to the new parliament. The writ runs thus:

> Elizabeth the Second by the grace of God, etc., to —— Greeting. Whereas by the advice of Our Council We have ordered a Parliament to be holden at Westminster on the —— day of —— next, We command you that, notice of the time and place of election being first duly given, you do cause election to be made according to law of —— member(s) to serve in Parliament for ——. And that you do cause

the name of such member when so elected whether he be present or absent, to be certified to Us in Our Chancery, without delay.

These returning officers then appoint a day for nominations in each constituency, when the names of candidates must be submitted, together with the signatures of eight supporters and a deposit of £150, which is forfeited by any candidate who receives less than one-eighth of the votes cast. If, as still happens occasionally, there is only one nomination, that candidate is declared duly elected: otherwise a day is appointed for voting—the same for the whole country.

Meanwhile each candidate is busy commending himself to his constituency. There are three recognized methods of doing this. One is the election address—a printed leaflet in which the candidate expresses his views on the political questions of the day and explains his qualifications for acting as the representative of the people he addresses: every elector receives this gratis through the post. Then there are casual contacts established by the use of posters —which, when they are cleverly drawn and worded, attract the eye of many voters who would not bother to read the address—and by canvassing. The candidate himself will tour every corner of the constituency by car, talking to all and sundry, while his supporters go from house to house, arguing his case. Lastly, there is the public meeting. Every hall and schoolroom is booked up at election time, and the police are often kept very busy preserving order in the vicinity of the meetings of an unpopular candidate. For although these meetings are attended mainly by those who would vote for him in any case, there will be heckling by opponents, who come in order to pose awkward questions

—and may incidentally give a candidate a good chance of proving his mettle. He may also try to increase his chances by bringing in leading politicians from outside the constituency to address these meetings on his behalf, though at the present day it is chiefly through their television appearances and broadcasts that the party leaders influence the prospects of the individual candidate.

Of election day itself we have already seen something. Suffice it to add that the polling stations are open all day (7 a.m. to 9 p.m.) so as to give the busiest workers time to record their votes, and that the boxes are then sealed up and conveyed to a central station, where their contents are carefully counted under the eye of the returning officer and the candidates with their agents. There is great competition to produce the earliest results. Most of the big towns make their announcement in the course of the night following election day, but rural constituencies, where the boxes have often to be conveyed long distances under guard, are not ready to do so until nearly twenty-four hours after the close of the poll. The scene ends with the successful candidate addressing the people from the town-hall balcony, his agent and canvassers wreathed in smiles, and a rather shorter and less delighted utterance from his defeated rival or rivals.

We have confined our attention to the procedure at a general election. This may be a convenient place to add that, when a member dies or otherwise vacates his seat during a parliament, he is replaced at a by-election. The procedure is much the same, except that more interest is generally taken by the public (and the newspapers) outside the constituency concerned, because the result may be held to indicate whether the government is keeping or losing favour.

3. THE FUNCTION OF PARTY

In all probability the reader has already noticed a striking omission in our account of elections and electioneering—nothing has been said about the parties, one of which nearly every candidate claims to represent. For although a few M.P.s call themselves Independents, 98 per cent (the figure is meant literally) belong to one or another of the great national parties, pre-eminently Conservative and Labour. One reason why this is so appears if we ask how candidates are chosen. Almost anyone is legally eligible, provided he is a British subject living in the United Kingdom: the exceptions are the obvious ones of minors, lunatics, persons serving a term of more than one year's imprisonment for treason or felony, and undischarged bankrupts; members of the house of lords (including Scottish peers represented by other peers); Anglican, Scottish Presbyterian, and Roman Catholic clergy; judges and stipendiary magistrates; and persons employed in the civil service, regular armed forces, and regular police. In practice, a candidate is normally someone singled out by reputation or ambition. In some instances they are local men who have distinguished themselves in local affairs as town councillors, active trade unionists, and so forth, and decide later on in life to stand for parliament. But the man who has served the locality is usually too attached to it by habit to aspire to a 'seat' (and a perhaps uncomfortable and certainly expensive place of residence) at Westminster: he leaves national politics to the ambitious younger man. The selection of a non-local candidate accordingly falls into the hands of the local political organization, which inevitably takes the shape of a branch of a national party, able to apply to headquarters for advice about a suitable person.

Beyond this, however, the party has three functions in connection with an election. Firstly, it keeps political feeling strong in the constituency between contests. This brings evil as well as good, because the local association and the agent are often eager to point out ways in which a prospective candidate may profitably 'nurse' the constituency, by giving ostentatious support to local charities, athletic clubs, etc. But, in a country where fully one-fifth of the voters do not exercise their rights at all, an association which sees to it that new voters are duly placed on the register and organizes meetings and fêtes at which political problems are discussed—mainly from the party point of view, of course—must be deemed to be on the whole advantageous to the public.

In the second place, it is easy to see that the party organization largely runs the actual election. In some cases the central fund of the party subsidizes candidates, particularly young men of great promise and limited means and those who carry the party flag, so to speak, in constituencies where the other side are overwhelmingly strong. But in any case it is the local committee of the party which provides the candidate with the bulk of his speakers, canvassers, committee members, and unpaid secretaries, without whom a lightning campaign, such as every general election involves, could not be undertaken at all.

But party has an even larger part to play than this implies. Candidates are not usually elected to parliament on account of their outstanding personal qualities—it might be better if they were. A man of great national or local celebrity has a 'pull'—a successful foreign secretary, for example, the head of a big trade union, or even a well-known county cricketer is thought to add dignity to a constituency: but in the main the candidate is elected as a cog in the party machine. The posters which say 'Vote for Jones' may add a list of the political views which he professes to hold or the name of the leader he professes to follow: in either event the principles or the leader means a party, which Jones, if elected, undertakes to support. On the whole, the leader is the more important emblem because a conspicuous individual appeals more easily to the popular imagination; but should the leader break with his party, the individual member may still be expected to follow the latter. In normal circumstances, however, the leader and the programme are indissolubly joined to the local organization, because the heads of the party closely watch the discussions of the annual conference, at which delegates from its local associations meet to air their views. More powerful still, perhaps, is the influence of the game, the feeling—which does much to keep interest in politics alive—that there are two well-defined sides, and that an act of desertion either by leader or by follower is to be regarded, not as an interesting intellectual phenomenon, but as tantamount to treachery.

4. THE MEMBER AND HIS CONSTITUENCY

Party likewise controls the activities of the duly elected member. We shall see more of this question in a later chapter: but the point may at once be raised, how far can the electors control the elected? The great eighteenth-century political thinker and writer, Edmund Burke, when member for Bristol, assured the electors in eloquent language that his duty to them was not to carry out their commands but to put his intellect at their service, by voting in parliament at his own unfettered discretion. But the problem nowadays is not altogether the same. Candidates offer numerous pledges, spontaneously in their election addresses, less spontaneously at their meetings, when devotees of all kinds of interests, from unilateral disarmament to anti-vivisection, extract promises that they will support appropriate measures. These pledges, however, are not taken very seriously, because the individual M.P. has to obey the party and, once arrived at Westminster, exercises little independent judgment. The rare exception occurs when a great many M.P.s have pledged their word on the same subject: on such occasions there may be a revolt against the party leaders, and something may really be done to honour the pledge. In general, it is unusual for the constituency to claim that its member obtained election under false pretences unless he actually changes his party allegiance.

What, then, does the constituency get from the member? In the first place, he will be expected to visit it and give some account of what is going on. That is why members receive a free railway pass between London and their constituencies, and why every Friday night (parliament does not sit on Saturdays) witnesses a considerable exodus to the country. Conversely, his constituents—in the shape of school parties, clubs, and deputations—expect sometimes to visit him, and to see the sights of Westminster under his guidance. More important is the ceaseless flow of correspondence. Every voter feels himself entitled to address the member upon any political question in which he happens to be interested. In a time of crisis these letters may arrive by hundreds and are a very valuable indication of public opinion: but woe betide the member who does not at least acknowledge the receipt of every one of these communications!

The voters will also be watching the newspapers to see that their representative is active. If parliament happens to have under consideration some bill (such as an electricity scheme or a plan for helping less prosperous areas) which directly concerns the locality, the member will be expected to speak on it. If not, it is open to him to prove his alertness by the questions he asks of ministers—above all, if a government department has committed some blunder in his constituency. Indeed, it is not unknown for members to ask questions with their own reputations in view rather than the answers. But, in the main, the connecting-link is simply this, that a member who ignores the presumed wishes of the electors too much will not be renominated by the local party organization at the next election. As such renomination is usually looked for, and as it is generally easier to retain an old seat than to capture a new one, this 'sanction' is fairly effective.

Subject to this limitation, we must admit that most M.P.s nowadays play a somewhat passive role in the working of the great parliamentary machine, the motive power of which is party.

III

THE HOUSES OF PARLIAMENT

1. HISTORICAL

IN the twentieth century a casual reference to 'parliament' may fairly safely be assumed to mean the house of commons: yet parliament originally meant the house of lords. Several indications of this remain, such as the fact that the royal assent to acts of parliament is declared in the lords, and not in the commons, and the practice by which the clerk of the house of lords is designated 'clerk of the parliaments'. It was not until the reign of Edward VI that the commons began to hold their discussions in official quarters within the Palace of Westminster or to record them in official journals; and the typical mediaeval member was a person who shrank from public life, and after reluctantly attending a single session which lasted only a few weeks would insist that it was someone else's turn to serve, if a parliament were to be summoned next year. He and his fellows, through the mouth of their Speaker, granted taxation and promoted bills, but the real power rested with the magnates. Their house, in contrast, though the numbers were still small, was already assuming something like its modern form—lords spiritual, which meant archbishops, bishops, and mitred abbots, and lords temporal, namely the heirs of those barons whom Edward I had summoned in 1295 and the holders of new peerages created by royal letters patent. The Lord Chancellor, from whom they received their writ of summons, was already the *ex officio* Speaker of the upper house, though the powers attaching to that position were (and are) much more limited than in the lower house.

Under the Tudors and Stuarts the commons gained in relative importance. They shared the general outlook of the Tudor sovereigns, assisted their policy (especially the reformation of religion), and acquired in consequence greater dignity and weight. It was at this time that their privileges (which they share with the house of lords) were beginning to be established, including freedom from arrest except on major charges so long as parliament is sitting, freedom of speech, and freedom of procedure. The liberty to discuss any matter at any time and in any way, which is the essential liberty of parliament, came to be protected eventually by the right to discipline, not only its own members, who may be suspended or expelled, but outside persons (such as newspaper editors), who may be imprisoned until the end of the session for offences against parliamentary privilege. Meanwhile, in Elizabeth I's reign privy councillors began to contest seats and regular 'parliament-men'— M.P.s who sat in several successive parliaments—made their appearance. The unwisdom of the Stuarts, on the other hand, gave the commons the chance to lead the national resistance—under Cromwell the house of lords was even for a time abolished—and the prime result of the Revolution of 1688, in which the struggle terminated, was to make the commons the visible masters of the state. We say 'visible' because, although public business was henceforth transacted in the lower rather than the upper house, individual peers controlled so many of the borough seats by their wealth that, up to the passage of the 1832 reform act, they exercised an invisible but decisive influence over the deliberations of the apparently more powerful commons.

The two centuries following the 'glorious revolution' saw parliament in its heyday of power. This was the period when the dogma of the sovereignty of parliament had most meaning. It had triumphed over the crown, and its authority was but rarely challenged by the people. Sir William Blackstone, the representative lawyer of the period, amplifies the theme in the measured language of his day: Parliament, he says,

> hath sovereign and uncontrollable authority in the making, confirming, enlarging, restraining, abrogating, repealing, reviving, and expounding of laws, concerning matters of all possible denominations, ecclesiastical or temporal, civil, military, maritime, or criminal: this being the place where that absolute despotic power, which must in all governments reside somewhere, is entrusted by the constitution of these kingdoms.[1]

In 1832 the balance of power passed definitely from the lords to the commons, but within fifty years of that date the practical authority of parliament as a whole began to wane—a process which seems still to continue.

One cause of this has been the growth of a new custom by which the cabinet, if defeated in the house of commons on an important question, instead of resigning holds a general election. A century ago, in the days of lord Palmerston, it commonly happened that the house exercised its power by procuring a change of ministry: but nowadays the knowledge that to attempt a change will involve a general election, with all its risk and trouble for the

[1] *Commentaries on the Laws of England* (1765), I, p. 160.

individual member, constrains the ministerial party to obey the ministers. Another, perhaps greater, change is due to the vastly increased pressure of business. A century ago parliament did well if it passed one law of first-rate importance in a session: consequently there was time for every private member to express his views as often as he liked. Indeed, the Speaker, that august official who presides over the debates and rules the house under its standing orders, had then no power to limit what was said in 'the best club in the world'. The modern thirst for legislation has changed all this. Time is carefully portioned out at the beginning of each session, and the period of discussion for any particular bill can be cut short by the closure, introduced into standing orders to stop obstruction by the Irish in 1881. In its simplest form this is a motion 'that the question be now put', which the Speaker may accept at any time if it has the backing of a majority which includes at least 100 members. More commonly there is agreement beforehand that the vote on certain stages in a bill must be taken at a fixed time (the 'guillotine') or that the Speaker or the chairman of a committee shall have power to jump over some clauses or amendments without allowing their discussion (the 'kangaroo'). Even so, some government bills get crowded out, while controversial measures proposed by private members stand practically no chance of being enacted (see p. 42).

Thus the powers of the commons are not so great as they seem. On the other side, it is important to notice that, in comparison with the powers of the lords, they have increased. This is the effect of the parliament act of 1911, passed after a controversy of the bitterness and magnitude which might be expected in the case of a constitutional change greater than any made since the revolutionary era of 1688–9. After a long period of quiescence the house of lords was aroused by the vigorous legislation of a Liberal government which came into office in 1905: a number of its measures were rejected, and even the budget, with which the lords did not customarily interfere, was voted down. To render such work impossible in future, the Parliament Act restricted the power of the lords to a suspensory veto. Any money bill certified as such by the Speaker can be held up by them for no more than one month; any ordinary bill could be held up for no more than two years if during that period it had passed through all stages in the house of commons three times over. An important limitation of this new power was involved in another clause, which said that parliament must be dissolved at least once in every five (instead of every seven) years, for a bill which passed the house of commons less than two years before an election was due could still be blocked by the lords until the electors had a chance to record their verdict on it. Even two years was too long in the view of a Labour government wishing to clear the way for controversial measures of nationalization, so in 1949 the second parliament act reduced the duration of the suspensory veto to a single year.

In practice, however, the lords, at any rate since 1914, have not actually fought measures to the bitter end. That may help to explain why proposals for 'ending or mending' their house, which were rife in 1911, have made very slow progress. The upper house of to-day consists of three distinct elements. There are the two archbishops of the [of Canterbury & York] established church and 24 of its bishops, namely those holding the sees of London, Durham, and Winchester, and the next in seniority of appointment. There are about 800 hereditary lay peers, including 16 elected every parliament to represent the peerage of Scotland and the last survivors of 28 peers elected before 1922 for life to represent the peerage of Ireland. This is, of course, the predominant element, but its general character is governed by the tendency for old titles to die out, while the Honours List twice annually may add new ones. More than half the present-day peers belong to creations made since the end of the first world war; the proportion whose titles date back beyond the lavish administrations of the younger Pitt (1783–1806) is almost insignificant. The third element is made up of life baronies—nine for law lords, whose presence has for many years been needed to enable the house to discharge its functions as a supreme court of appeal, and a small number of others (first made available in 1958) for men and women of distinction who are selected by the prime minister, after consultation with the opposition, for their ability to 'help in the working of parliament'.

The house of lords has thus come to represent wealth and to a considerable extent public service more than blue blood. As for the work it does, three useful functions may be pointed out. Although their amendments to bills are liable to be overruled in the last resort under the parliament act procedure, the examination of new laws by the lords often leads to improvements in detail agreed with the commons. Then there is the fact that the allocation of cabinet posts to members of the upper house makes it possible to have a proportion of ministers who are less heavily burdened with parliamentary duties. Finally, there is no doubt that the lords' debates, though often dull and occasionally futile, enable some problems to be ventilated for which the commons either cannot or will not spare time. The colonies, the armed services, education, and road traffic regulations are examples of subjects of great importance, where the lords can always muster experts and the commons for party reasons may sometimes fight shy of a debate.

Another landmark in the history of parliament, which dates from the same year as the parliament act, was the reintroduction of the payment of M.P.s. In the middle ages they had commonly received wages from their constituents, but this practice had fallen into disuse as soon as membership came to be a valued social distinction. Indeed, it was originally the members of parliament bringing their wives and daughters with them to the capital for the short annual session—from February to July or early August— that provided the nucleus for the fashionable London Season. The changing financial status of M.P.s, particularly but by no means exclusively those of the newly formed Labour party, made the provision of salaries (1911) and travelling allowances (1924), chargeable upon the national finances, a necessary item of public expenditure. A more remarkable illustration of the pace of social change is the fact that since the second world war the payment of daily attendance money for their services has become acceptable to members of the house of lords.

2. CONTROL OF THE PUBLIC PURSE

The main original duty, which the members of the house of commons were summoned to fulfil, was to vote taxes to the king: the taxes, in his view, would be paid more readily if representatives of the 'communities' of the realm had agreed to them beforehand. Assenting to taxation is still one of their main functions, as year by year the queen's ministers bring before the house the requirements of the different services. But it is important to notice that money is granted only in accordance with those stated requirements, for a standing order of the house of commons prescribes that no sum of public money can be voted for any purpose, however small and casual, except on the proposal of a minister of the crown. This prevents the frittering away of funds upon local objects, which might gratify the constituents of particular members and to which other members might hesitate not to accede, or even upon national objects of a generous but imprudent description.

Before 31 March—the day on which the government's financial year ends—the requirements of each department for the following year are laid before the house as the estimates, covering the costs of defence, civil service expenditure of all kinds, and the smaller amounts needed for the machinery by which revenue is collected. Some of them will be individually examined by sub-committees of the select committee on estimates, but the Committee of Supply, which is a committee of the whole house sitting with relaxed formalities under the chairman of committees, has a quite different function. It meets on 26 weekly 'supply days' from February to August, and as the requirements of each department are brought up in turn, members take it as their opportunity to review its policy and administration, a common form of procedure being to propose a small nominal reduction in the salary of the minister concerned.

The upshot is that the committee of supply eventually passes a series of votes, each of which allots precise sums (even to shillings and pence in some cases) for particular services. At the end of the allotted period a second committee of the whole house, called the Committee of Ways and Means, formally embodies them—together with any votes which there has not been time to discuss—in the annual appropriation bill, which is passed by the commons and sent up to the lords, who must approve it (under the provisions of the parliament act) within one month. But the final stage is really the audit of the ensuing expenditure by the comptroller and auditor general, whose staff authorize the payment of money to the treasury for the work of the departments day by day, and will eventually certify to the parliamentary committee of public accounts that the money has actually been spent in accordance with the appropriation. Nevertheless, scandals of extravagance are more easily exposed than rectified.

The committee of ways and means is so called because it used to find the 'ways and means' of providing each item of supply from the proceeds of a particular tax. This is no longer done, because the proceeds of all taxes are now paid into a single consolidated fund at the Bank of England, from which the appropriation act referred to above enables the government to draw the sums agreed to for particular purposes in the course of the proceedings of the committee of supply. The other function of the committee of ways and means is much more important, namely the authorization of new taxes. It is before this committee that the chancellor of the exchequer opens his budget (the word means a brief-case) in early April, in which he explains how far revenue and expenditure have balanced in the financial year that has just ended, and what changes will be necessary to meet the expenditure of the new financial year. If the estimates are 'up', he may announce a higher rate of income tax, a heavier duty on tea, tariff changes, or the flotation of a government loan. Thus the budget speech is usually a long and arduous performance for the chancellor, and provides material for keen debate, though the alterations which the committee makes in his proposals are likely to be small. The new taxes are eventually embodied in a single Finance Bill.

Such is the general outline of the system, though there are of course many special arrangements for bridging the gap between the presentation of the estimates and budget and the legal enactment of the proposals they contain. The departments obtain regular votes on account, and a statute of 1913 enables the taxes proposed in the budget to be collected provisionally for four months on the authority of a resolution. A more important device of the same kind is the vote of credit, by which parliament grants the government money in case of emergency, such as war or the imminent danger of war. There can be no campaigning without cash, so the need to get a vote of credit deters the government from adopting a bellicose policy which may prove unpopular with parliament.

Nevertheless, the financial control of parliament is admittedly imperfect. A portion of the public expenditure is charged permanently upon the consolidated fund and does not come up for review annually. This includes the interest and sinking fund on the national debt and such smaller items as the civil list, which supports the royal family, and the salaries of the lord chancellor, Speaker, and high court judges. Conversely, a large part of the revenue—which, however, does not include income tax and tea duty—is likewise levied under permanent acts of parliament. This is probably as it should be, since time is limited and some matters, such as the actions of judges, are better left unreviewed. A much more serious matter is the apparent impotence of the house of commons in face of government proposals. Standing orders forbid a private member to increase a vote of supply; the technical difficulties in the way of proposing alternative schemes of taxation are enormous; and the total expenditure nowadays is so vast that only a small part of the field can be covered in the time allotted to discussion of the estimates. As far back as 1918 a select committee reported that in a period of 25 years no single estimate had ever been reduced by direct action of the house of commons taken on financial grounds.

The estimated revenue and expenditure for a single year, as set out in the budget speech of the chancellor of the exchequer on 4 April 1960, are worth studying from

ESTIMATED REVENUE, 1960-1

	(£,000 omitted)
From Inland Revenue	
Income Tax	2,478,000
Surtax	190,000
Death Duties	239,000
Stamps	110,000
Profits Tax, etc.	256,000
Total from Inland Revenue	3,273,000
Customs	1,458,630
Excise	950,150
Motor Vehicle Duties	113,000
Total from Taxes	5,794,780
Post Office (net revenue)	4,000
Broadcast Receiving Licences	39,000
Miscellaneous	142,000
Total Revenue.	5,979,780

ESTIMATED EXPENDITURE, 1960-1

(£,000 omitted)

Interest and Management of National Debt	640,000
Sinking Funds	40,000
Payments to Northern Ireland Exchequer	89,000
Total	**769,000**

Supply Services—Defence

War Office Votes	487,450
Navy Votes	397,500
Air Votes	529,460
Ministry of Aviation (Defence)	198,850
Ministry of Defence	16,570
Total	**1,629,830**

Supply Services—Civil

i. Central Government and Finance	18,568
ii. Commonwealth and Foreign	103,154
iii. Home Department, Law and Justice	103,211
iv. Education and Broadcasting	212,389
v. Health, Housing, and Local Government	1,335,033
vi. Trade, Labour, and Aviation	92,804
vii. Common Services (Works, Stationery, etc.)	89,941
viii. Agriculture and Food	325,168
ix. Transport, Power, and Industrial Research	237,524
x. Pensions, National Insurance, and National Assistance	631,199

Tax Collection

Customs, Excise, and Inland Revenue	69,340
Supplementary Provision	71,000
Total Expenditure	**5,676,161**
Surplus (estimates in excess of expenditure)	303,619

many points of view, among them their size: the total sums involved are roughly eight times as large as they were a quarter of a century ago, which means that the state now takes and expends at least twice as much as then, even after allowance is made for the greatly reduced purchasing power of money.

3. LEGISLATION

The fact that the parliaments of many countries are termed legislatures or legislative assemblies may remind us that their primary function, in these days when government activity plays such a large part in life, is to pass laws. The greater part of every parliamentary day—or rather evening, for business at Westminster does not begin until 2.30 p.m.—is devoted to the discussion of bills or to financial business, the results of which will likewise be embodied in a law.

The process of legislation, which is regulated not by statute law but by the standing orders of each house, is as follows. Every bill must be introduced by a member, on whose proposal it is declared to have been read (there is no actual reading and no discussion at this stage): the bill is then printed and circulated to members. The next stage is the Second Reading, when—if the matter is of importance—a big debate will take place, at the end of which a formal motion that the bill be read a second time must be carried: otherwise the bill falls to the ground. If successful so far, it will be referred to a committee, either one of six regular Standing Committees of about fifty members or—in the case of an important and controversial measure—a committee of the whole house. Committee is the stage for detailed discussion and amendment, as distinct from debate on the principle of the measure, which takes place at the second reading and again at the Third Reading, which follows when the bill has been reported from the committee to the house. Amendment is also possible at the time of reporting, so there are in all five stages, ending with the vote on the third reading.

These five stages must then be repeated in the other house, a bill which originates in the commons (as most do) being sent 'up', and a bill from the lords sent 'down'. If the second house wishes to alter the bill, its amendments must be considered also in the house where it originated and be accepted there: otherwise the bill (except under the parliament act procedure) still falls to the ground. If, however, it is successful at all these points within the limits of a single session (about a twelvemonth) the royal assent will be declared by commissioners according to ancient ceremonial, and the bill at last becomes the law of the land.

This description applies to all public bills, that is, bills concerning any general or public interest, but their actual fate depends very largely upon a further sub-division between Government Bills and bills which private members wish to bring forward. Under the present system the latter are almost always crowded out. Ten Fridays in each session is the portion of parliamentary time set aside for their discussion, when bills may be brought forward by members who are lucky in the ballot. But they rarely get much further than the second reading, especially those which happen to be introduced near the crowded end of the session. The only other chance is given by a standing order known as the Ten-Minute Rule, under which brief statements can be made about a Private Member's Bill for which no time has been otherwise provided. Indeed, the only real profit that results from discussion of such bills is that sometimes they are adopted by the government, which either finds additional time for them, so that they may be passed, or reintroduces them as government measures in the following session. This is a great weakness of the system, for private members' bills have often embraced far-sighted proposals, particularly on non-party subjects: daylight saving, for example, figured in a private member's bill eight years before the government adopted it in 1916.

If a private supporter of the government cannot hope to bring forward his own bills, much less can a member of the opposition, whose bills will be automatically crushed by the government majority. What, then, is the use of the opposition in parliament regarded as a legislative body? The answer is that standing orders always provide as much time as possible for criticism of the government's proposals. They are, almost invariably, strongly challenged both on principle and in detail, which means that the government spokesman, with his eye on the public outside as well as on his numerically inferior opponents within the house, is compelled either to justify or to amend his schemes. There are few measures which do not in some way benefit by this.

Lastly, there is a separate class known as Private Bills, promoted by some private interest, such as a railway authority seeking powers to buy land. They are usually sponsored by a municipality, corporation, or limited company, but there is nothing (except the high cost) to prevent any citizen from seeking parliamentary powers to do something otherwise illegal with his own land or property. Private bills receive three readings in the ordinary way, but in their case the vital stage is the committee, consisting in the commons of four members and in the lords of five, whose task is to consider arguments for and against the bill put by specially briefed lawyers (hence the high cost). Once such a bill has been accepted, as it were judicially, by a committee in each house—the house of lords, having more leisure, shares fully in this work—the other stages in both houses become more or less a formality. It may be added that considerations of time as well as money make people prefer to get whatever powers they need granted them through a government department instead. If the department is satisfied by the case made out at a public local enquiry it will list the proposed order, perhaps with others, in a schedule attached to a special type of quasi-private bill, which, being sponsored in this way, is usually enacted without difficulty.

4. THE PARLIAMENTARY DAY

The member of parliament is not always engaged upon the task of legislation, either in the committee rooms or on the floor of the house. If we were seated in one of the galleries of the house of commons we should see members continually entering and leaving the chamber, whispering to each other or (with a more important air) to the ministers on the front bench, while a few would-be orators, notes in hand, wait to catch the Speaker's eye, that is to say, to be called upon by him to address the not very crowded benches. Government and opposition members have their place on opposite sides of the house, which they leave from time to time to stream out and in again through the two lobbies, where they are counted to record a vote on each motion (such as the amendments to some bill) put from the chair. But before the division, as it is called, is actually taken, bells ring throughout the whole palace of Westminster, giving six minutes for the numerous members who are not in their places to hurry in to vote, prompted by their party's whip. For notices stating the expected time of the division will have been sent out in advance, with up to three underlinings to measure its importance, and the party officials who send them out—whippers-in or Whips—keep a very sharp eye on the response, the ultimate penalty for refusal to obey the whip being exclusion from the party. A free vote takes place only on very rare occasions, when some important issue is recognized as lying outside party politics: a proposed revision of the church of England prayer-book and the demand to end capital punishment are well-known examples.

However, the time of the zealous member is taken up in other aspects of parliamentary business, sometimes more profitable than detailed discussion of bills which the government majority means to force through, however eloquently phrased and well-founded the objections. One of these is the regular daily period of questions, which (except on Fridays, when the house meets and rises earlier) follow immediately upon the assembly of the house of commons and the reading of prayers by the Speaker's chaplain. Two days' notice must be given: with this restriction any member may ask any question he likes of any minister with reference to the conduct of his department. As we should expect, the questions are very numerous, but the situation is eased by the practice of circulating printed answers to the majority of them, a verbal answer being given where the matter is of great interest or a member specially asks for it. In some cases, too, the question never actually reaches the house, because the minister who would have to answer it prefers to forestall possible trouble by acting at once in response to a member's letter.

This system is a most valuable safeguard for the liberty of the subject. To give two examples—a British subject has been unjustly treated abroad and, having no money or influence, cannot obtain redress: a question is put to the foreign secretary; patriots are indignant; the British consul is immediately ordered to act. Or a small but ancient school is about to be closed as part of some huge scheme of reorganization: there is strong local feeling in favour of the school; the minister of education is questioned; the school survives.

Another valuable activity is general discussion of policy, quite apart from any new law. There are various forms under which such discussions take place: one is for a member to get the Speaker's leave to move the adjournment of the house on a matter of urgent public importance. If a minimum of forty members support him by rising in their places, or the motion is carried by a majority, a general discussion of policy follows the same day at a later hour. In the house of lords, which has more leisure for this kind of thing, the common form is for the opposition to move that papers be laid before the house on such and such a subject, which motion, with house of lords politeness, is withdrawn when the desired discussion is ended. More generally, we may say that the state of the nation—the trend of foreign policy, for instance, or an increase in unemployment—can be debated at any time by arrangement made between the leaders on both sides of the house.

Such a general debate also takes place automatically at the beginning of each new session, when the queen, from the throne in the house of lords, reads her speech, which is actually a compilation by her ministers, setting forth in very general language their plans for the session. In reply to the Queen's Speech, the house of commons votes a loyal address thanking Her Majesty, to which opposition speakers always propose to add expressions of regret that various measures, which they would prefer, are not included in the ministers' plans. This enables much to be said on both sides of the house, though the passing of any amendment proposed by the opposition would normally mean that the government must resign.

This brings us to the last, and perhaps the most important, function of the house of commons—the making of ministries. It is said that nowadays 'the two capital realities are the Ministry and the electors', meaning that a ministry depends primarily upon the support it appears to enjoy in the country at large, and only secondarily upon support in the house of commons. In three respects, however, the attitude of the house is of direct importance to ministers. Firstly, it provides a reserve machinery for deposing a ministry. At the present time it is usual for ministers to resign immediately after a general election has shown that their opponents have a majority in the country, and not otherwise: but if a ministry in such a case refused to resign, an amendment to the address, a refusal of money supplies, or a direct vote of censure by the house of commons would be the means employed to extrude them. Secondly, it is in parliament, and pre-eminently in the commons, that men publicly establish their fitness as individuals to become ministers. It is still rare for high cabinet rank to be accorded to anyone, however distinguished, who has not made some reputation there in debate or committee. Lastly, the day-to-day attitude of members towards the government acts as a barometer of success, which weighs with ministers at least as much as the opinion of the press: for members of parliament are sufficiently close to affairs of state to form sober judgments, and at the same time sufficiently in touch with their various constituencies to know what the country is thinking, so that they are often in a position to act as a real guide to their titular masters, Her Majesty's Government. This is particularly true in times of grave emergency, as in May 1940, when it was the withdrawal of support by Conservative back-benchers that caused the replacement of Neville Chamberlain as war leader by (Sir) Winston Churchill.

IV

THE CABINET

1. PRIVY COUNCIL AND CABINET

THE history of the cabinet is the history of a transformation. What had once been a committee of royal advisers, such as was to be found in most of the European monarchies, became a parliamentary party committee discharging nominally the same duties but in practice ruling the country—an arrangement which was for a long time peculiar to Great Britain. The name Cabinet, which implies a meeting in the king's private study or 'cabinet', referred originally to nothing more definite than the small body of intimates picked out of the full council, whom the later Stuarts were wont to consult in preference to the privy council as used by their predecessors. For the council had become too large and formal for real discussion to take place at its meetings, and committees of councillors were the obvious substitute. Then came the revolution of 1688 and the consequent increase in the power of parliament, which made it prudent for the foreigner, William III, to make a show at least of admitting to the inner circle of his advisers men whose party connections enabled them to control the houses in the royal interest. Queen Anne, being a woman, carried this a stage further by letting the inner circle decide policy where her predecessor tolerated only advice: though she dismissed them, when their war policy caused them to forfeit her rather fickle favour, *before* a general election was held to show that they had also forfeited the favour of the electorate. Queen Anne also anticipated modern developments by associating cabinet membership with the holding of particular offices of state. Nevertheless, the change from royal advisers to ruling committee was so far from completion that she continued to preside at all regular cabinet meetings.

Broadly speaking, then, the cabinet, as we know it, began with the Hanoverian dynasty in 1714.

For one thing, within four years the sovereign had entirely ceased to attend its meetings and was replaced as chairman by a leading minister, whose office approximated more and more to that which we know as the premiership. The cabinet also became more definitely a party institution, in which every member had to belong to one of the two houses and to one and the same party in the house; and as a party committee the members must stand or fall together, united in the advice which they gave to the king and united in the responsibility which they all accepted for the political activities of each. Nevertheless we must be careful not to exaggerate: the crown was not a mere cipher in relation to the cabinet. Such a leader as Sir Robert Walpole felt himself to be very much the king's servant, dismissible as such; George III's cabinets more than once contained members of a discordant party, whose presence the king demanded; George IV tried to get the members of a cabinet to give individual opinions on the merits of Canning's foreign policy, in the vain hope of confronting the minister with the hostility of his colleagues; and William IV once or perhaps twice contemplated the dismissal of a cabinet which had the support of the house of commons and the electorate.

Thus the complete theory and practice of cabinet government, roughly traced in the eighteenth century, were never really systematized before the reign of Queen Victoria. Under Peel, Disraeli, and Gladstone its workings became more uniform: indeed, one of the classic expositions of the subject is still a chapter in the life of Walpole, written by one of Gladstone's colleagues (Morley) with his master's assistance. Meanwhile, the privy council, from which the cabinet had sprung, continued to increase its unwieldy numbers: in the eighteenth century it had ceased to advise, in the nineteenth the title of privy councillor and the prefix 'Right Honourable' came to be awarded as a political honour comparable, perhaps, to a baronetcy. The total membership has grown slowly to about 280.

What of twentieth-century history still in the making? Under the pressure of more, and more urgent, business the cabinet has already undergone great changes. Its normal size has grown from a total of 12 or fewer members to one of 18 or more, while during both world wars prime ministers have found it necessary to form a smaller war cabinet, functioning inside the main body, to ensure swift action in emergency. In wartime, too, the cabinet sacrificed its normal party basis in the effort to achieve national solidarity. A more lasting change has been the setting-up (by Lloyd George in 1916) of a secretariat—a small body of civil servants who prepare the agenda of each cabinet meeting for the prime minister's approval, record the discussions and especially the conclusions arrived at, and see that decisions become known to those who have to carry them out. This Cabinet Office, modelled upon the small secretariat which since 1904 had served the committee of imperial defence, is a good example of a move towards systematization, which enables a present-day cabinet to take in its stride a variety and multiplicity of tasks which would have appalled not merely Sir Robert Walpole but Gladstone or Asquith.

This we shall see more clearly when we consider the cabinet at work. But we must first return to the privy council, heir to a great tradition, and remark its three surviving functions. First, it is a source of committees—chief of these the cabinet itself, for every member is formally admitted to the cabinet by his taking the oath of office of a privy councillor. There is the great judicial committee, to which we shall refer later; there was—in the vital periods preceding the two world wars—the above-mentioned committee of imperial defence, whose duties have been absorbed by the cabinet itself; and a privy council committee is also responsible for the forward-looking activities of the department of scientific and industrial research. Second, there are quite frequently executive meetings of the council, held by the queen in person with the clerk and some three or four other members, which are the proper occasions for the authorization of all kinds of official orders in council, ranging from minute instructions under some special statute to the documents whereby parliament itself is summoned. Thirdly, the privy council holds its only full meeting on the occasion of an accession, when, after the more crowded assembly (see p. 4) at which the accession proclamation is ordered, the privy councillors remain to hear a declaration from the new sovereign and to be the first subjects to take the oath of allegiance.

2. THE WORK OF A CABINET MINISTER

The term 'cabinet minister' may remind us that, while the cabinet is the committee of advisers, the ministry is the name used for a rather different institution, namely, the body of 'placemen' or, as we now say, officials, who see that what has been decided upon is actually carried out in the administration of the country. As these are offices of dignity, power, and emolument, the inner circle of advisers, described above, tended from the first to occupy the foremost places themselves.

To take, for example, the Conservative cabinet which held office at the end of 1960, we find that it contained the following 20 ministers:

Prime Minister (who was also First Lord of the Treasury)
Secretary of State for Foreign Affairs
Chancellor of the Exchequer
Lord President of the Council (who was also Minister for Science)
Lord Chancellor
Lord Privy Seal
Secretaries of State for the Home Department, Commonwealth Relations, Colonies, and Scotland
Ministers of Labour; Housing and Local Government (who was also Minister for Welsh Affairs); Agriculture, Fisheries, and Food; Education; Transport; Aviation; and Defence
President of the Board of Trade
Chancellor of the Duchy of Lancaster
Paymaster-General

The full ministry, however, included some sixty other persons. Fifteen of these were ministers of cabinet rank not having seats in the cabinet: the first lord of the admiralty and the secretaries of state for war and air might be said to be represented in the cabinet by other ministers; others, such as the minister of works or of pensions and national insurance, had charge of departments which were for the moment of lesser importance; and Ministers of State, instituted twenty years before as cabinet representatives in the various theatres of war, formed a small category of assistant ministers under another and rather misleading name. The rest of the number was made up of the government's four law officers (attorney-general and solicitor-general and their counterparts for Scotland); the financial secretary to the treasury and the various parliamentary secretaries and under-secretaries, one of whom serves under each minister in his department; and the parliamentary secretary and five junior lords of the treasury, the high-sounding title of the Government Whips in the house of commons.

Although the rapid growth in the activities of the modern state has resulted in a situation in which there are far more departments than there are cabinet ministers, it remains true that for the average cabinet minister a heavy load of departmental work is one of his three great responsibilities. The offices vary considerably in dignity from time to time, though the foreign office and the exchequer are for obvious reasons always key positions: in 1960 the leader of the house of commons (see p. 60), who was clearly the second man in the government, preferred the work of the home office. The president of the council and the lord privy seal, who together with the chancellor of the duchy of Lancaster and the paymaster-general have the smallest departmental duties, are often senior colleagues to whom a prime minister delegates important tasks of planning or a general oversight of affairs. The lord chancellor, who held a post akin to that of the modern prime minister in much earlier days, still takes precedence of him officially and, in virtue of his double role as head of the judiciary—he recommends all appointments of judges—and presiding dignitary of the house of lords, has also a higher salary. In practice, at least three other ministers must either be chosen from, or elevated to, the peerage, so as to represent the government in the house of lords. There used also to be a difference in dignity between a secretaryship of state, derived from the ancient office of King's Secretary, and one of the newer ministries, but that has largely disappeared; all regular cabinet offices except the premiership and the lord chancellorship now carry with them the same official salary, and—with the exceptions already indicated—the tendency is for the status of each post to vary with the importance of the work in which a particular department is at the moment engaged.

The actual routine work of any department is performed, not by the minister in charge, but by a staff of civil servants, whose activities we shall study in a later chapter: but the final responsibility must rest with him. Few of us would readily change places with a man who has to guide the policy of such a many-sided organization as, say, the home office or the ministry of education, especially when we take into account the average minister's inexperience. For it is safe to say that, whenever a new cabinet is formed, a clear majority of its members (sometimes nearly every man) are appointed to offices which are wholly new to them. It is a tribute to the industry and force of character of the average minister, as well as to the efficiency of the civil service, that the great departments perform their tasks with anything like reasonable success.

Yet that which we have been describing constitutes only one of the three functions of a cabinet minister. The second may be dismissed quite briefly. He owes his position to the fact that he is a more or less prominent supporter of that political party which for the time being has a majority of supporters in the house of commons, and which is therefore called upon to 'form a government'. In all probability his standing with the party has been one of the main inducements to the prime minister to give him place. Accordingly, the cabinet minister throughout his term of office is expected to be considering what measures will be popular with the party, and to give the party his help by assiduous attendance at Westminster and frequent and effective participation in debate.

Nevertheless, the third function is the vital one. We may rest assured that the new member, whom the summons invites to 'a meeting of Her Majesty's servants', is aware that the cabinet, in which is concentrated authority over the United Kingdom and its dependent territories, is something more than a colloguing of party chiefs. A rigid custom constrains all members to keep silence about cabinet discussions and decisions, which rule may only be broken (with permission) when a minister, having quarrelled with his colleagues and resigned office, wishes to explain his conduct to parliament. The custom is obviously advantageous to the party, which would rapidly disintegrate if the disputes of its leaders were habitually made public, but it finds its legal basis in that privy council oath of secrecy which every cabinet minister has sworn. Accordingly, we cannot say much about the informal discussion of public affairs and the more formal business of making decisions, which constitute the regular task of the cabinet. But one outstanding feature is the nominal equality of all members, both as regards the right to be heard and, in case of a division, the voting-power: senior and junior members each count for one and for one only. Nevertheless, it may be surmised that senior members sitting near the prime minister at the head of the table are more readily audible in counsel, and voting is said to be very rarely required.

The cabinet may meet anywhere, but the famous cabinet room at 10 Downing Street and the prime minister's room in the houses of parliament are the two usual places. A list of business to be transacted is circulated to members beforehand in the official boxes of state papers which are conveyed to ministers almost daily, wherever they happen to be. There may be some major question of policy ripe for decision, in which case it is likely that a small cabinet committee (containing three or four of the most influential ministers) has drafted a proposal in advance. A bill may be submitted, which expert lawyers known as treasury counsel have been instructed to put into legal form beforehand, but which must be carefully examined before it goes to parliament; or, in the case of any project entailing new public expenditure, there will be a careful memorandum from the treasury itself. There may also be a discussion of foreign affairs or Commonwealth relations, based on reports from ambassadors and high commissioners abroad. All in all, it is easy to understand that the weekly meetings of the cabinet, which are suspended only during the parliamentary recesses (especially the long autumn recess), have often to be supplemented at times of crisis or when the budget is impending.

3. THE PRIME MINISTER

So far as any office in Great Britain can be compared at all with the American presidency or with the chairmanship of the council of ministers in the Soviet Union, it is obviously the office of prime minister. In the beginning, as we have seen, he was the person who took charge of cabinet meetings when they ceased to be attended by the sovereign; and, since the cabinet by that time was representative of one party, the person who took charge of the meetings was normally the party chief as well. But the growth of democracy has added a third aspect to the dignity of prime minister. Ordinary men and women—most of us, in fact—are appealed to by a person more easily than by a set of principles: at an election we vote for the party that supports So-and-so as leader, and at a crisis we look for a solution, not to the party principles or programme, but to the character of the leader who carries the party with him. This tendency may well be deplorable, but the fact remains that a modern general election is sometimes hardly more than a demonstration of popular confidence in one man, who is thus nominated prime minister in effect by the electorate.

The prime minister is, of course, actually appointed by the sovereign, whose hand he kisses on accepting office, and of whom he takes leave on resigning. He has an official residence at 10 Downing Street, which was presented to Sir Robert Walpole by George II; and since 1906 he has been placed fourth in the official table of precedence, ranking next after the two English archbishops and the lord chancellor. But his practical authority is even greater than the nominal position suggests.

The Prime Minister

In the first place, the prime minister is the only link between the other ministers and the sovereign. Apart from the 'cabinet conclusions', which are drawn up by the cabinet secretariat, the sovereign has no knowledge of cabinet discussions, except what the prime minister may choose to impart. Moreover, the prime minister selects his colleagues and can, if necessary, compel any of them to resign. The fact that his cabinet has to be a collection of men prominent in the party, some of whom have probably held cabinet rank before, limits his choice: but at least he divides the offices at his discretion and decides which of the younger and less known men deserve promotion. And, when he himself resigns office, the cabinet is automatically dissolved. Hence a vast general power of supervision:

> The duties of the Prime Minister, if one may use the expression, surround the Cabinet. He stands in a sense between it and all the other forces in the state with which it may come into contact, and he even stands between it and its own members. Matters of exceptional importance ought to be brought to his attention before they are discussed in the cabinet: and any differences that may arise between any two ministers, or the departments over which they preside, should be submitted to him for decision, subject, of course, to a possible appeal to the cabinet. He is supposed to exercise a general supervision over all the departments. Nothing of moment that relates to the general policy of the government, or that may affect seriously the efficiency of the service, ought to be transacted without his advice.[1]

In the second place, the premier has vast powers of patronage. All members of the ministry, down to the second church estates commissioner or the vice-chamberlain of the royal household, are chosen by him. It is on his

[1] A. L. Lowell: *Government of England*, I, p. 69.

recommendation that the sovereign appoints archbishops and bishops, other high dignitaries of the established church, and the regius professors at Oxford and Cambridge. His wishes must also be consulted with regard to the highest posts, not only in the civil service, but in the navy, army, and air force: announcements of this kind, if of special public interest, are commonly made direct from 10 Downing Street. Furthermore, the premier has a presumed right to nominate to any new office under the crown which parliament may choose to create.

In the third place, the prime minister used generally to be leader of the commons, that is to say, he arranged the plan of business for the session; took charge when any question of misconduct in the house arose; and assiduously watched the debates so as to encourage government supporters and ensure as smooth a passage as possible for government measures. This particular burden, involving long hours of unprofitable waiting on the treasury bench (where ministers sit), is now felt to be excessive. In old days the prime minister was sometimes saved by being or becoming a member of the house of lords, but this is held to involve a dangerous affront to the modern democratic idea. A more acceptable alternative, which has been regularly adopted for the past twenty years or so, is the appointment of a separate Leader of the House of Commons, who rids the prime minister of a tiresome responsibility, while the latter remains free to intervene in day-to-day business when necessary.

In the last place, the prime minister has enormous reserve powers in time of crisis. A great debating assembly, such as the house of commons, loses public confidence when instant action is called for. Even the cabinet with its score of members is believed to talk too much. The wise sovereign is less disposed than ever at such a time to intervene with direct advice or to transfer authority. Then the prime minister, whether in the days of the elder Pitt or in those of Winston Churchill, becomes a kind of temporary dictator; consults habitually with a handful of colleagues only; and depends directly upon the sometimes misplaced but always understandable patriotic fervour of the people, which sees the national cause embodied in his person.

4. HER MAJESTY'S OPPOSITION

One all-important distinction between our form of government and that of some other countries to-day is that the British cabinet never even in theory represents all the best talents in the nation. At any given moment there are good men, whose experience and character would make them more suitable as home secretary or as foreign secretary than the actual occupants of those offices, excluded by the fact that they belong to the party which for that moment is in a minority in the state. Not only so, but the men who are in office consume much of their time in considering, not what it is best to do, but what the party situation will allow them to do—a good bill *may* benefit the state, but it *must* be one which will elude effective attack by the opposition. And the prime minister himself is commonly regarded with complete mistrust—and a very vocal mistrust at that—by at least one-third of the electorate.

It is not enough to say that this is a system under which we have long flourished, that the very phrase 'Her Majesty's Opposition' is a century old, and that in recent years the leader of the opposition has even been allotted an official salary. How does an institution seemingly so inimical to national unity in fact serve the common interest?

The answer is threefold: firstly, the opposition leaders are all the time acquiring experience through the work of opposing, and there are some mistakes at least which they are learning to avoid. This is extremely important, because the existence of a reasonably efficient alternative administration alone gives the country real liberty of choice. At the same time, opposition orators keep the government up to the mark. They are never slow to remind its members of election promises which they are failing to keep, or to point out that new measures which were not foreshadowed at election time clearly lack the 'mandate of the people'. There are few bills which do not gain something through the intensive criticism to which the system subjects them, while the exposure of any positive slackness or corruption in the conduct of government business is an ever-present threat. And lastly, strong, well-disciplined attacks by the opposition put the government on their mettle and bring to light the best as well as the worst features in their conduct of affairs.

Above all, the party aspect of politics, which makes it a great game of Ins and Outs, helps to keep public interest awake. England was for centuries fortunate in the existence of two parties, each of which had its roots deep in the national life and each of which brought forward great leaders, who through party served the state. Between the world wars the position was less satisfactory: three parties, indeed, contended for power, but of the three only the Conservatives were ever able to secure a clear majority in the house of commons so as to carry their programme through. A dramatic reversal of fortune came in 1945, and in the next few years keen argument attended the establishment by the Labour party of the welfare state. In the later 1950s, however, it was chiefly the dilemmas of foreign policy that kept controversy alive. Apathy remains a greater danger to free institutions than partisanship.

Nevertheless, it is desirable to state clearly the conditions upon which the smooth working of party government depends. Firstly, there must be a readiness to regard an issue as closed—the situation would be impossible if each new administration spent its time undoing the measures passed by its opponents. Secondly, compromise must be in the air—the parliamentary machine cannot work properly if every action of the government is challenged and every minister pursued by a furious vendetta, as in the days when fallen ministers might even be impeached by their successors. Thirdly, changes of government must not be too frequent: unless a party is strong enough to carry its measures over a period of four or five years it can follow out no proper constructive policy and will discredit both itself and the system.

Finally, there must be a symbol of national unity and tradition to fire the imagination of the common man, to keep the party struggle within bounds, and to remind opposing cabinets, as they succeed one another, of their common obligations to the state. The parliamentary convention which, in all ordinary circumstances, forbids the name of the sovereign to be mentioned in debate, lest it should imply that the sovereign took sides in politics, illustrates a general belief that to personify national unity is both the natural and the necessary function of the British monarchy.

V

THE MONARCHY

1. THE BASIS OF LAW AND TRADITION

THE crown of England is above all the symbol of the continuity of English history, and for that reason the study of its powers, their rise and fall, has some meaning for us today. In the Norman period the powers of government were nearly all concentrated in the hands of the king, and although the later middle ages witnessed the transference of many of them—to the king's judges, for instance—a resolute sovereign continued to make his wishes effective in every department of state. This was still true under the Tudors, whose privy council existed to advise but not to replace the king. There followed the classic struggle between crown and parliament, from which the English parliament, having enlisted the religious sympathies of the majority of the people on its side, emerged triumphant in 1689. With William III and Mary II the modern history of the monarchy begins.

The evolution of the cabinet was, as we have seen, the main achievement of the next one and a half centuries. But from the point of view from which we are now considering it, the most remarkable episode of that long period was George III's attempted revival of personal authority over his parliamentary ministers, which came to a disastrous end with our failure in the American war in

1782. This, however, left virtually no trace upon the constitution. It is more to our purpose to notice the sustained interest in foreign policy—the fact that our kings were also electors of Hanover was one cause and their marriages with German princesses perhaps another. A sustained interest in the army likewise distinguished the royal house for many generations. George II was the last king to command in person, but his younger son, the duke of Cumberland, crushed the Jacobites at Culloden; George III's second son, the duke of York, was an important army reformer; and Queen Victoria's cousin, the reactionary duke of Cambridge, served as commander-in-chief for almost two-thirds of her long reign. But the outstanding feature is the survival of political influence on the negative side: in the early nineteenth century the cabinet still required the king's leave to introduce any contentious legislation. That this was no mere formality is shown by the fall of Pitt in 1801, when George III refused to allow catholic emancipation; the dismissal of the Grenville ministry upon the same issue in 1807; and the importance of William IV's doubts and hesitations in the story of the reform bill crisis. Lastly, we must add the unpopularity which seemed then to be an attribute of the crown. George I was a complete stranger; George II vain and slightly ridiculous; George III in a reign of sixty years covered the whole gamut from popular young hero to hated despot and thence to pitied madman; and George IV and his brother (though the older of the two was shrewder than the books often suggest) were guilty of grave excesses to which their debts, constituting a heavy drain on the public purse, all too frequently drew attention.

The reign of Queen Victoria passed through several distinct phases. From the outset her youth and innocence gave the court a dignity and an exemplary moral tone which it retained throughout. In the 'fifties, the period when Palmerston was virtually dismissed the foreign office at the royal behest and prince Albert was given the title of prince consort by letters patent, the influence of the monarchy underwent some revival, especially in foreign affairs. But the prince was an earnest student of the constitution as well as of foreign policy, and would never have been a party to any attempt to dictate to the representatives of the people. After his early death in 1861 the queen largely abandoned her social functions and was for a time decidedly unpopular, an unpopularity which she kept alive in some quarters by her determined hostility—within broad limits of constitutional propriety—towards the later policies and the personality of Gladstone. Finally, in old age she re-emerged as the symbol of imperial unity: a formidable little old lady, slowing down the rate of progress in domestic affairs, zealously using her influence among the numerous crowned heads who were her relations to advance—so far as she understood them—our interests abroad, and always deserving that last tribute by which her birthday is now Commonwealth Day.

For the twentieth century much must still be left to conjecture. Even for the reign of Edward VII the relevant sources come only gradually to the light of day, and those of his son and grandsons are to be studied chiefly through the officially authorized biographies and the duke of Windsor's own book, *A King's Story*. But it is generally held that the powers of the monarchy, left largely intact during the venerable old age of Queen Victoria, were diminished under her son in spite of his protests: for example, the right to veto the inclusion of an individual in a ministry finally disappeared at this time. As for the eventful quarter-century over which George V dutifully presided, it seems evident that the first world war gave him a great chance to stand out as representative of a people under strain, of which his character (and that of his consort, Queen Mary) enabled full use to be made. In his last years some of that veneration, which had been felt for his grandmother, was felt for him, and he appears to have won an influence over men which more than replaced any decline in formal powers. Edward VIII, who as prince of Wales had done much to extend the influence of the royal house overseas, reigned too briefly and too unhappily to leave much positive mark on his inheritance. His brother prince Albert's decision to adopt the style of George VI signified the adoption of a programme as well as a name, for in spite of impaired health and a speech impediment, he earned much the same reputation as his father for a strict attention to his constitutional duties. Again we may hazard the guess that in the difficult circumstances of war and its bitter aftermath this gave more weight to the king's position than could have been gained by any outstanding gifts of intellect. Such are some of the latest contributions to the long tradition of monarchical practice which was inherited by Queen Elizabeth II.

The legal, as distinct from the political, history of the monarchy may be dealt with very rapidly. In 1689 the Bill of Rights debarred from succeeding to the throne any Roman Catholic heir and any heir married to a Roman Catholic. In 1701 the Act of Settlement further restricted the succession to 'the princess Sophia and the heirs of her body being Protestant', a line which has neither failed nor shown signs of failing. But an important regency act of 1937 for the first time made permanent provision for a regent, who shall act while the sovereign is under the age

of 18 years or is certified by high officials of state to be
rendered incapable of discharging his or her duties by any
mental or physical disability. The regent was to be the
person of full age next in succession to the throne, but the
law was later modified (1953) in order that the duke of
Edinburgh might hold office on behalf of his child, as it
were by right of fatherhood.

The same legislation of 1937 and 1953 provides for the
increasingly common situation, in which the duties of the
sovereign, particularly those in relation to other member
states of the Commonwealth, necessitate a prolonged ab-
sence from the United Kingdom. The royal powers are
then entrusted for routine purposes to the sovereign's
consort, if available, and the next four heirs to the throne
excluding minors, with the addition of Queen Elizabeth
the queen mother.

2. THE POWERS OF THE QUEEN

British kingship, like most other parts of our ancient Constitution, has a very modern side to it. Our King, in virtue
of his descent and of his office, is the living representative of
our national history. So far from concealing the popular
character of our institutions . . . he brings it into prominence. He is not the leader of a party, nor the representative
of a class: he is the chief of a nation . . . He is everybody's
King.

The sentiments which lord Balfour, a statesman of long
experience, expressed in introducing a new edition of
Bagehot's *English Constitution* shortly after the first world
war remain true to-day. Everybody shares emotionally,
though with infinite varieties of taste and feeling, in the
events of a reign—an accession or a jubilee, a birth, a mar-

riage, or a death within the royal house. Parties and classes disappear into the background of our thoughts, as we contemplate, on the one hand, the long and eventful history which links Alfred with Elizabeth II, and on the other hand, the personality of a sovereign, for which it is so much easier to feel interest and sympathy than for a prosaic organization such as a party. In that connection we must consider that radio and television, which now make the voice and features of the queen familiar in every home, have added notably to the potential effectiveness of modern monarchy. Thus the queen's first source of power is that she, more than anyone else, can remind us that we are one nation.

Secondly, we must notice the influence which the sovereign still wields as 'Head of Society'. All titles and decorations are awarded on her behalf; and although the lists of honours for the New Year and at the queen's birthday are compiled under the authority of the prime minister of the United Kingdom or any other member state concerned, the queen's wishes, if she feels strongly about any proposed award, must be carefully considered. Moreover, there are three orders which remain in the personal gift of the sovereign—the knighthood of the garter, which is the oldest and most prized of the orders of chivalry; the order of merit, which speaks for itself; and the Victorian order, awarded generally for specific services to the royal family. Of wider importance is the distinction which the queen or any royal personage can confer upon an institution or society by a royal visit or by permission to cite a royal name as patron. From a university to a hospital, there is the same desire to obtain this hallmark of worth; and in these days of highly organized and competitive publicity, the success of any charitable enterprise depends to an enormous extent upon its ability to attract the royal interest. Once this is gained, it will not lack other patrons and patronesses.

At the present day the greatly diminished influence of the sovereign upon foreign affairs is mainly of the same kind. Although our ambassadors and ministers abroad are treated ceremonially as her personal representatives, it is safe to say that the queen has no control whatever over the policies they are instructed to pursue. What she can do is to add the personal touch, of which the organs of publicity will make much in any land. An attack is made upon the life of a national leader or a whole people is afflicted by some catastrophe of nature—the queen will cable her sympathy. A big international conference assembles in London —the queen may open it and perhaps entertain the delegates at Buckingham Palace. Or it may be desirable to cement relations between Britain and some other power: an official visit from or to the queen, with all its attendant festivities, tends to create mutual feelings of interest and amity, to which the personalities of the queen and her consort make a very striking contribution.

Then the observant newspaper reader will be aware that part of the queen's time is given up to audiences. Many of these are formal in character, as when a foreign ambassador presents his credentials or a bishop swears fealty or a governor is received on appointment to a colony, but to be received by the sovereign is also a significant social distinction. An innovation of the present reign has been the series of small-scale parties with about a dozen guests, at which the queen has made the acquaintance of leading figures from various walks of life, while the vast official royal occasions, round which the London season used to revolve, fall slowly into abeyance. To some extent this suggests a widening of the royal interests as well as of the social circles to which a democratic sovereign must pay conscientious attention. But her most important dealings are of course with the prime minister, for whom a weekly audience is now the common practice.

Bagehot—upon whose sage observations King George VI had made extensive notes—declared that in relation to the prime minister the sovereign had three rights, namely 'the right to be consulted, the right to encourage, the right to warn'. The sovereign is certainly consulted less fully now than a century ago, when there used to be a taking of the royal pleasure before any official appointment could be announced and dispatches were commonly communicated before they were sent abroad. But the powers of encouragement and discouragement retain their vigour because, as Bagehot clearly showed, the sovereign has two advantages over the premier, which may outweigh the fact that the latter is inevitably a man of far more than average ability, and the sovereign probably not. One advantage is the aura of reverence surrounding the royal office, which must add weight to the opinions of a monarch and deters the minister from directly refuting the royal arguments. The cultivation of a deferential attitude, however, may now be somewhat outmoded. But the other, unfailing advantage enjoyed by the monarch lies in the permanence of his position vis-à-vis a more or less temporary minister, which means that accumulated experience makes him a mentor whom a wise premier is not merely obliged, but positively desires, to consult. He knows what mistakes were made by previous ministers, and probably why they made them.

An interesting illustration is provided by what happened in July 1945, when the transfer of power from Churchill to Attlee occurred during the Potsdam conference of the

Allies, for which representation of the foreign office must be provided. The king's diary suggests that he took the initiative in raising the question of the foreign secretaryship with the new prime minister as soon as the latter had kissed hands on receiving appointment. In the words of a memorandum made by the Private Secretary immediately afterwards, 'Mr. Attlee mentioned to the King that he was thinking of appointing Mr. Dalton to be his foreign secretary. His Majesty begged him to think carefully about this, and suggested that Mr. Bevin would be a better choice.'[1] In so far as the wishes of King George VI may at least unconsciously have affected lord Attlee's final decision, he may be said to have exercised a most important influence upon the trend of British foreign policy in the following momentous five years.

But, in addition to these various kinds of political influence, the British monarchy retains some vestiges of political power. The power of creating peers, so as to swamp opposition to ministers in the house of lords, is one of these, but the passage of the two parliament acts makes it improbable that the present queen would ever feel called upon to destroy the effect of a veto which is merely suspensive. It is more likely that she would use her influence (as Queen Victoria twice did) to effect a compromise between the upper house and the government of the day, and, failing that, she would almost certainly require a general election to show the will of the country before she acted.

This brings us to a more real issue: has the sovereign the right to dissolve, or to refuse to dissolve, parliament in defiance of the wishes and advice of responsible ministers?

[1] Quoted by Sir John W. Wheeler-Bennett: *King George VI His Life and Reign* (1958), p. 638.

His control (within a five-year limit) of the duration of a parliament is the weapon which enables a prime minister to cow factions among his own supporters in the house, who fear the trouble of a dissolution, and to disregard press campaigns and other popular follies outside, since they cannot force him to dissolve. It therefore follows that, if the sovereign withheld this control from any prime minister, the government would be driven to resign. The question thus becomes: in what circumstances may the sovereign dismiss a ministry? In two cases, surely, and two alone: one is when their demand for a dissolution occurs with unreasonable frequency and is likely, if acceded to, to bring the democratic system into contempt; the other (a more probable situation) is when their refusal to advise a dissolution is inspired by the knowledge that the general trend of their policy runs contrary to the wishes of their proper masters, the electors.

> The Queen's function, it is suggested, is to see that the Constitution functions in the normal manner. It functions in the normal manner so long as the electors are asked to decide between competing parties at intervals of reasonable length. She would be justified in refusing to assent to a policy which subverted the democratic basis of the Constitution, by unnecessary or indefinite prolongations of the life of parliament, by a gerrymandering of the constituencies in the interests of one party, or by fundamental modification of the electoral system to the same end. She would not be justified in other circumstances.[1]

On this showing there is a third type of situation, one which is bound to recur from time to time, calling for political action on the part of the sovereign. In the normal

[1] Sir I. Jennings: *Cabinet Government* (3rd edition, 1959), p. 412.

course of events the resignation of the ministry and the formal surrender of their powers into the royal hands involve only a comparatively simple transaction, for the sovereign sends at once for the leader of the opposition, which has proved too strong for the outgoing premier to withstand, and invites him to form a new government. Or alternatively, if a prime minister resigns while his party remains in power, the person to be invited to form the new government will normally be indicated by his prominence in the party, though we must note in passing that the post of deputy prime minister, which existed during the second world war and until the final retirement of Sir Winston Churchill in 1955, has never been officially recognized by the sovereign. The assignment of offices may take a week or so to complete, and in the meantime the retiring ministers retain their existing positions.

But if nobody is clearly designated, the constitution ceases to 'function in the normal manner' and it is for the sovereign to choose—a situation which is liable to arise whenever the house of commons majority contains two or more approximately equal parties or groups, or if it has two or more leaders of roughly equal standing. It is sometimes maintained that it is the royal duty in such a case to seek the advice of the outgoing prime minister. But if his opponents are to succeed him, he may lack intimate knowledge of the individuals concerned, while if the choice has to fall on one of his own former colleagues, his representations may be intimate but not dispassionate. There is also the possibility of a prime minister having died in office. Accordingly, in the given circumstances the sovereign may be expected to conduct his own negotiations, consulting elder statesmen and others at his own— or his private secretary's—discretion. Thus George V came to add a precedent of some significance to our constitutional traditions by his action in 1923, when he decided not to select a prime minister who was a member of the house of lords. In January 1957 it was publicly stated that the queen's choice of Mr. Macmillan to succeed Sir Anthony Eden was made after consultation with lord Salisbury (himself perhaps a victim of the precedent just mentioned) and the veteran Sir Winston Churchill.

3. THE QUEEN AND THE COMMONWEALTH

The founders of the British Empire in the seventeenth century carried their allegiance with them wherever they went: even the Puritans who crossed the ocean to escape from the persecutions of Laud and Wentworth in church and state regarded themselves without question as still the subjects of King Charles. The converse proposition also holds true, for the independence of America began with the repudiation of allegiance to George III.

The new empire which grew up largely in the reign of Victoria was likewise one in which the idea of an all-embracing monarchy played a central part. It is true that the practice of responsible self-government along the lines of the Durham report of 1839 was quickly extended from its first home in Canada to British settlers in Australasia and South Africa. It is also true that the governors of such settlements were nominees of the cabinet of the United Kingdom, which supported the use of the governor's power of 'reserving' bills for further consideration by the crown in order to give the home government a modicum of control over the wilder actions of what were then still called 'colonial' ministers and legislatures. But governors, who were often noblemen of ancient lineage and high fortune, gave great dignity and considerable importance to their position as direct representatives of the distant sovereign under whose aegis development had begun. In 1876, too, the prestige of the monarchy appeared to be notably enhanced through the assumption by act of parliament of the title of emperor of India or Kaisar-i-Hind, a name associated with the grand moguls of the past which won the veneration of Indian princes, if not the affection of the Indian peoples. As for the ever-growing throng of more primitive tribes and peoples, which in the closing decades of the century were assembled under the union jack—the 'dominion over palm and pine' of Kipling's Recessional, a *pièce d'occasion* of 1897—in their eyes the Great White Queen was something more than the symbol of their oppressor. She was also thought of as a chieftain who could grant protection, such as the Basutos had sought against the Boers; who would personally receive their petitions; and to whom homage should be paid, as in the calculated pageantry of her two jubilees. Thus the British Empire, like nearly all the great empires of the past, grew around a throne.

The vital part played by the self-governing dominions in the first world war led inevitably to a revaluation of their constitutional status, expressed in the Balfour declaration of 1926, which the Imperial Conference formally ratified in 1931 (see p. 187). No less inevitable, for the historical reasons outlined above, was the assertion then made that Britain and the autonomous equal communities of the empire overseas were all 'united by a common allegiance to the crown'. Though the principle was clear, the practice involved some difficulties. Since the dominions now had an exact equality of status with the United Kingdom, a governor-general must be appointed strictly in accordance with the advice tendered to the sovereign by the prime minister of the dominion concerned. This left the door open to occasional unwise appointments from inside the dominion of keen political partisans and persons otherwise unfitted by character or experience to represent the crown. The actions of a governor-general, too, must now be guided by the sovereign without reference to advisers in the United Kingdom. While this gave the king a very important new activity, it was one in which he had to move with extreme caution for want of expert independent information on dominion affairs. Moreover, any modification in the legal position of the royal house now required the express consent of the United Kingdom and each of six dominion governments. This applied to the regency acts already named. More significant is the fact that in December 1936 Edward VIII's decision to abdicate involved a temporary though purely formal disruption of the Commonwealth: for the reign was legally terminated in the Union of South Africa one day before, and in the Irish Free State one day after, its termination by acts of parliament elsewhere. This temporary division of the crown may be said to have foreshadowed the view which found expression on the accession of Elizabeth II in 1953, namely that her crowns and titles are separate in the different member states, though there is a common law of succession.

Meanwhile, George VI's reign had seen the first important withdrawal from allegiance since the unhappy events in America in the early years of George III. For the southern Irish the British crown was a symbol of past servitude and old injustices which continued to rankle. Not content with whittling away the powers and dignity of the governor-generalship, in 1937 they adopted a republican constitution by plebiscite, but left in existence an 'external association' with the monarchy for purely formal purposes such as the accrediting of diplomatic representatives. Although this compromise arrangement helped them to demonstrate their practical independence by remaining neutral during the war years which followed, the sequel was secession. It was at this very time that the dominion of India—the larger of the two fractions into which the Indian Empire had been divided according to the wishes of its inhabitants in 1947—was preparing its new constitution. Again for historical reasons the name of republic was a shibboleth, and it seemed likely that the power of India would be lost to the Commonwealth. The term Head of the Commonwealth was then adopted, involving the peoples of India in no more than the recognition of a purely symbolic dignity attaching to the British sovereign in all parts of the Commonwealth by virtue of his being accepted as king in some parts of it.

The compromise solution which the member states of the Commonwealth approved for India has proved a fertile precedent. Thus Pakistan has become an Islamic republic, while Malaya has carried the new possibility further by instituting its own elective monarchy, to be held by the sultans of the federation in turn. The only proviso is that a member state which changes its constitution in this way must obtain the agreement of the other member states to its remaining within the Commonwealth.

What, then, are the functions that the sovereign now exercises outside the United Kingdom, either as 'queen of her other realms and territories' or as 'head of the commonwealth'? Where the queen is recognized only as head of the Commonwealth, she is not personally represented in any way in the government of the country, though a good deal of interest may nevertheless be taken in reports of royal speeches and in news of the queen and her family. But wherever she is queen, a governor-general or governor still acts as her representative and the government is carried on in her name. How far this is more than a purely nominal matter depends nowadays largely upon the human factor—the degree to which a particular representative is sensitive to the royal standpoint and the degree to which any particular people welcomes its expression. Except in a supreme emergency it may be assumed that the political activities of a governor-general are if anything even more strictly circumscribed by present-day constitutional convention than are the dealings of the sovereign with her ministers in the United Kingdom. In a colonial dependency, on the other hand, the governor is a much more significant figure. He is, of course, acting on behalf of the sovereign, whose dignity may be exhibited in a good deal of pomp and circumstance. But except in purely social matters, what he does is strictly controlled by the colonial office, in the case of any dependency of the United Kingdom, or by the equivalent authority in some other member state.

The sum total is so small that, if communications remained as they were in Queen Victoria's day, the result as an influence to bind together a vast commonwealth would be almost negligible. But broadcasting and television, to say nothing of books, magazines, and newspapers, give the queen and her family a place in myriads of homes: the remoter its situation, the greater her potential influence. The queen is brought into direct contact with many visitors to London, ranging from prime ministers to students, the last-named at a most impressionable age. She in turn accepts an obligation to visit and if possible revisit countries overseas, perhaps opening a session of parliament or presiding over a meeting of her privy councillors within the member state. How considerable an innovation this is may be found by comparing the journeys of Queen Elizabeth II in the first few years of her reign with the last 16 years of George V, during which the king and his consort spent only five weeks outside Great Britain. But for the wearer of a crown which is declared to be both common and divisible there is a further possibility, that regular royal residences may be established in other member states and the United Kingdom at some periods be entrusted to a governor-general. This would consummate the evolution to complete equality, and might open up new spheres of influence to the historic British monarchy.

4. POWERS OF THE CROWN

Hitherto we have been considering the activities of the sovereign as a person: but a great many other activities go on in the royal name—activities in which personal wishes play no part, but which, in the eyes of the law, appertain to the wearer of the crown. In many cases they are things which our earlier kings did with full responsibility, which caused trouble in parliament, and which after 1688 or 1714 came to be done more satisfactorily by the king's ministers acting in his name. A single maxim may show how completely the sovereign as a person has been obliterated from the general business of government. 'The king can do no wrong' meant originally that the king cannot be prosecuted in law courts which are, in a sense, 'his' courts: it has come to mean conversely that, whatever (political) wrong is done in the king's name, some other person, normally a minister of the crown, must bear the responsibility.

A great many activities of the crown result nowadays from acts of parliament, which provide that orders in council shall be issued to fill in the technical or variable details of the law in question. Under a foot and mouth disease act, for instance, an order may be required to make the provisions of the law applicable to any particular district; or elaborate regulations under an act may require to be submitted to the council before they become valid. This is the main business of the meetings of three or four councillors with the queen and the clerk, referred to above: the titles of orders are read out, the queen declares them 'Approved', and the clerk affixes the appropriate seal and his signature.

More interest, however, attaches to the use of the royal prerogative, that is to say, of those powers of the crown which it possesses by unbroken tradition, acknowledged as such in the law courts, and not by statute. Much of this finds expression in merely conventional forms, such as the business of signing every army officer's commission, to which Queen Victoria devoted endless hours; the document under the great seal conveying the royal assent to legislation; and the order for the issue of writs, which, as has been previously explained, is the first step in the summoning of a new parliament. The formal language of this last perhaps merits quotation.

> At the Court at ——, the —— day of ——, 19——. Present, the Queen's Most Excellent Majesty in Council. Her Majesty having been this day pleased by Her Royal Proclamation to dissolve the present Parliament and to declare the calling of another, is hereby further pleased, by and with the advice of her Privy Council, to order that the Right

Honourable the Lord High Chancellor ... do upon notice of this Her Majesty's order, forthwith cause writs to be issued in due form and according to law for the calling of a new Parliament, to meet at the City of Westminster: which writs are to be returnable on —— day, the —— day of— 19——.

The fact that such documents are both numerous and indispensable constitutes one reason why the regency act of 1937, already mentioned, provided for the automatic appointment of councillors of state to substitute for the action of the sovereign in matters of this kind. For the lack of such regular provision in the event of illness was found inconvenient on two occasions towards the end of the reign of King George V.

But the prerogative also includes some powers more valuable to ministers—and more debatable. Such in the past was the prerogative of pardon, but this has not been used for some centuries in the case of political offences. The prerogative gives ministers power to naturalize aliens, or to give a whole community a new status, as by incorporating a borough or authorizing the conversion of a college into a university—nearly all our modern universities were established without the intervention of parliament. These are powers which might be abused: others, the use of which has at times been actually challenged, include the power of ceding territory, the legislative power in territory obtained by conquest or cession, the power of dealing with enemy trade and property in time of war, and the power of taking measures otherwise illegal in order to prevent an invasion of the realm. In the war of 1914–18 ministers used the prerogative with such vigour that on one occasion (*A.-G.* v. *Wilts United Dairies*) they were successfully challenged for an attempt to impose taxation without consent of parliament in defiance of the Petition of Right of 1628!

Lastly, there is the power of appointment to all kinds of offices under the crown. Not all the offices to which the government of the day appoints are, strictly speaking, under the crown: the members of the boards that govern nationalized industries, for example, though appointed (and in some circumstances dismissible) by a minister, hold office under statute. But civil servants of every grade, down to the Whitehall messenger with a crown on his uniform and the driver of the monogrammed mail van, as well as all members of the armed forces, owe both privileges and liabilities to their position under the shadow of the royal prerogative, as we shall see later (p. 108).

VI

THE QUEEN'S COURTS

1. THEIR EVOLUTION

ONE of the original functions of a king in any country was to judge disputes between his subjects and declare what constituted offences against the whole community. Accordingly, we find that in the primitive England over which William the Conqueror held sway the king himself acted as judge in important cases which were brought to court. A slight trace of this historical background of our legal system survives in the prerogative of pardon, still exercised by the home secretary in the name of the crown. But broadly speaking the judicial powers of the crown have been dissipated in four distinct stages.

The first—a process which had begun in the time of the Conqueror—was the hearing of cases at the royal court by the council, acting for the king. This, we may note in passing, survives in the functions of the judicial committee of the privy council, the judgments of which still technically take the form of recommendations to the crown. Secondly, the hearing of cases devolved upon special councillors, who travelled round the country in the king's name, pronouncing judgments as authoritative as if they had been given at court and in the royal presence. This system, which was firmly established in the reign of Henry II (1154–89), is the system of judges riding their circuits to hold the local assizes. Thirdly, there was the problem of hard cases, where the rigid administration of law would work unfairly and it was presumed to be the king's beneficent task, if he were petitioned, to interfere. In the thirteenth century this, too, became separate from the royal office and was transferred to the chancellor in his capacity as 'keeper of the king's conscience'. Hence came a separate system of law, known as equity, which was administered in the special court of chancery. Lastly, the judges ceased to be under the control of the crown. To this day a judge entering his court is treated as the direct representative of the crown, before whom all must stand in deferential silence. But since 1714 his patent of office has conferred the appointment 'during good behaviour'; he can be removed from it only by joint address of both houses of parliament to the crown; and his salary is fixed, so that no pressure can be brought to bear on him. When in 1931 a special law was passed to enable the salaries of all government servants, from the premier downwards, to be reduced as an economy measure, the judges protested against their inclusion as involving an encroachment upon this absolute independence.

Side by side with the courts there has evolved the system of law which they administer. At the present time this consists mainly of statutes enacted by parliament—a series which stretches back to the land laws of Edward I and even to Magna Carta, lying beyond the origin of parliament. But the making of statutes to govern all kinds of activities is largely a new idea: new laws were never numerous until the nineteenth century, and if we go back to the middle ages, when the sessions of parliament were very much shorter, it is obvious that they must have been very few indeed. How, then, did the judges decide cases?

The answer is twofold. On the one hand they relied upon general principles or maxims of law, derived partly from the earlier Roman law which they had studied, and partly from legal customs which they found already widely in force as they travelled the country. On the other hand they relied upon decisions already given, claiming that if they were considered narrowly enough they would always shed light upon a new problem, quite apart from any reference to general principles. Such is the origin of common law, which nowadays consists of case law—the records of decided cases upon which a judge bases any new decision not precisely covered by statute law. But the name really means 'law (i.e. custom) common to all parts of the country', which may serve to remind us that the judges once depended upon local assistance in all their work.

Before the age of royal judges all cases which were not important enough to be brought before the king in person were decided locally, for the most part in the county court, but also in feudal courts held by the lord of the manor. When the judges and assizes were instituted, the king (partly for the sake of collecting fines) wished to make these royal courts the more popular and efficient. Hence the use of two instruments, which have had a great history. One was a jury sworn to present criminal offences (i.e. produce the offenders) before the royal judge. This is the origin of the grand jury, containing the leading men of the county, which until 1933 continued to examine the cases to be brought at assizes and certify that there was enough evidence to warrant a hearing. The other is our most distinctive legal institution, the Petty Jury. In the reign of Henry II the petty jury was a body of twelve witnesses who decided cases of land ownership before a royal judge from their own knowledge, a method which won favour because of its expedition. But by the end of the middle ages it had emerged as the modern jury of twelve ordinary men, who hear evidence and a judge's summing-up—and then declare a verdict of guilty or not guilty, which to condemn must be unanimous.

Our legal system has been very conservative, that is to say, great changes have been made slowly and reluctantly, however urgently they were needed. One main reason for this we also inherit from the middle ages, namely the four inns of court, to one or another of which every barrister must belong, and from among the members of which all judges are chosen. The inn is a close fellowship or society: in such an environment ancient traditions flourish, and the very fact that such a community exists makes it difficult to modernize the law. This is clearly shown by what happened in the seventeenth century, when the early Stuart kings tried to establish new courts of their own, administering a new and often more efficient law upon the Roman model. The result was to throw the common lawyers on the side of parliament, which contributed largely to the defeat of Charles I. From the time of Charles II onwards kings left the common law courts severely alone, with the result that abuses accumulated and they became a by-word for inefficiency and dilatoriness. For hundreds of years England was governed mainly through local courts held by justices of the peace, local gentry who had long been entrusted with legal powers and were advanced by the Tudors to be a kind of local dictators. In the eighteenth century J.P.s were usually reactionary, often ignorant, and sometimes corrupt, but the higher courts rarely interfered with them; and it was not until 1873 that the judicature act marked the real modernization of our legal institutions.

G

The reform of that year completely reorganized the courts and removed the crowning absurdity of the old system, which was the hard and fast line drawn between statute and common law, on the one hand, and equity on the other. The latter had grown from its informal beginnings in the thirteenth century into an elaborate set of rules administered in chancery, which included such principles as the following:

> Equity will not suffer a wrong to be without a remedy.
> He who seeks equity must do equity.
> Delay defeats equity.
> Equality is equity.
> Equity looks to the intent, rather than to the form.

To obtain the application even of such common-sense ideas as these a case had had to pass to and fro between the two sets of courts: but the new system amalgamated them into a single high court, any division of which could administer both common law and equity. Where the two conflicted, equity was to prevail. This marks the final triumph of ideas which Jeremy Bentham had preached to unwilling ears in the reign of George IV, and which earlier reformers in parliament, such as lord Brougham, had spent long years endeavouring to translate into action.

2. THE COURTS OF LAW TO-DAY

Most of us, when we think of legal matters at all, think in terms of criminal charges, that is to say, police prosecutions (though they may also be started by private persons) for some alleged breach of the law of the land. If the case is of major public importance, the director of public prosecutions will be concerned, and the crown may even be represented by the attorney-general. We will therefore consider first the administration of the criminal law, which applies to all such cases, beginning with the courts of first instance.

If, in the opinion of the police, they have caught you more or less in the act of committing a serious crime, the proceedings may begin with your immediate arrest. But it is more usual for the police to proceed by laying an information before a magistrate, who will probably have a summons issued, requiring you to appear in court on a day named; or he may issue a warrant of arrest, if he thinks this necessary to secure your due appearance. In any event, the case will probably be heard by justices of the peace, unpaid amateur officials who are appointed by the lord chancellor on the advice of a special local committee. Every county, county borough, or other large town has its own commission of the peace, in which a considerable number of leading citizens are named for this purpose. Two or more sit at a time—there is usually a regular rota—in each petty sessional division (of these there are more than a thousand in all), and in populous areas petty sessions, now renamed officially the Magistrates' Court, meets daily. Two functions are there discharged—the punishment of minor offences by imprisonment for not more than six months and/or a fine not exceeding £100; and the preliminary examination of more serious crimes, to see whether the evidence warrants the commitment of the accused for fuller trial elsewhere. In some cases, however, a person accused of a serious crime has the option of a summary trial at petty sessions, if he prefers. A Juvenile Court is a form of magistrates' court, first introduced in 1908, which sits separately and with the minimum of publicity so that accused persons under 17 years of age may not be contaminated by association with adult criminals.

But the justices of the peace also hold for each county a more important court known as Quarter Sessions, which sits four times a year (sometimes at different centres) and is attended by all active magistrates. There the larger body hears appeals against decisions made at petty sessions and deals with the graver class, known as indictable offences, in the trial of which the court has the help of a jury. Quarter sessions cannot, indeed, try cases of murder and manslaughter or others for which the penalty may be penal servitude for life, but it does in fact handle about two-thirds of all indictable offences.

This would be a matter for surprise and perhaps alarm, if the law administered in these courts were the law as interpreted by amateurs pure and simple. There are three important safeguards. The justices never act without the assistance of their clerk, who is a trained solicitor, and at quarter sessions they are always expertly advised on the law by the officer of that court, known as the clerk of the peace for the county. Secondly, in the large towns they are often superseded by professional justices of two types. Stipendiary (and metropolitan) magistrates can hold a magistrates' court without the presence of another justice and in fact do most of the day-to-day business which in a large town is often difficult to handle. In those boroughs which have a separate commission of the peace a Recorder, chosen from among barristers of some standing, pays periodic visits for the conduct of quarter sessions; in Liverpool and Manchester he presides over a special Crown Court, which also conducts assizes. Both stipendiary magistrates and recorders are appointed by the crown. Thirdly, there is the power of revising and censoring all activities of the justices of the peace, which is freely exercised by the high court, to which we now turn.

The high court of justice and the court of appeal were both created by the act of 1873, which came into force two years later. But the High Court, although it discharges many of its functions at the law courts in the Strand, is strictly speaking neither a place nor even an assembly of judges—it is a list of as many as 48 judges, who try cases either singly or in groups. For purposes of criminal law administration, which provides the work of more than half of them, they form the Queen's Bench Division of the high court under the presidency of the lord chief justice. The gravest crimes usually come before them at assizes, which one or two judges, travelling one of the seven circuits into which the country is divided, hold three times a year in most county towns and other important or convenient centres. Juries are employed as at quarter sessions, the main difference lying in the fact that Her Majesty's judge is empowered to impose all sentences which the law may authorize. In the London area, however, the business is too great to be dealt with by the ordinary system of assizes, so a central criminal court has been instituted, which sits almost continuously under a judge at the Old Bailey; and cases from the provinces are sometimes transferred to this court to escape local prejudice.

There is no general right of appeal against the verdict given by a jury on the facts of a criminal case. But three judges of the queen's bench division sitting together constitute a Court of Criminal Appeal, before which a convicted criminal (through his advisers) may not only argue that the law in his case has been misinterpreted, but may also ask leave to appeal to the court upon the facts, on the ground that the jury has acted on wrong information.

Nevertheless, the number of appeals to this court, except against capital sentences, is not very large, because the court is empowered to increase, as well as diminish or quash, a sentence imposed by a lower court. Above the court of criminal appeal, and concerning itself exclusively with questions of law, there is finally the house of lords, which for legal purposes is composed of the lord chancellor, ex-lord chancellors and ex-judges who happen to be peers, and nine lords of appeal in ordinary, experienced judges who are given life peerages expressly for this purpose. But it is a curious reflection that it is only a political convention and no law which deters nearly eight hundred other peers of the realm, having no judicial qualifications whatever, from entering this most august court and taking an active part in its proceedings!

However, criminal cases on points of law require a certificate of their importance from the attorney-general before they can reach the house of lords, which is mainly concerned with civil suits, to which we now turn. When one citizen sues another, with the object of maintaining his private rights, usually by exacting some pecuniary compensation, an action for a small amount may take place in a County Court. This, like its ancient predecessor of the same name, is a local court, but the two are entirely unrelated: the modern county courts were instituted by act of parliament in 1846 and are presided over by a special class of county court judges ('His Honour'), nearly 70 in number, each with his own circuit of courts. At the county court the dispute will be decided by the judge himself, juries having now fallen into disuse. But an appeal will usually lie from the county court to the court of appeal (described below), and, if the sum at stake is large, the suit will begin in the high court: these are considerations that deter people of limited means from commencing actions against their neighbours. Such a high court case may be tried either by a judge on circuit at assizes or at the law courts in London: the use of a jury is mainly at the judge's discretion and has now become uncommon, but in commercial cases tried in the City of London it is still possible for either side to apply for a Special Jury of persons who are better qualified than the ordinary jury to grasp the details of a complicated case. From the high court an appeal lies, for those who can afford it, to the Court of Appeal, consisting of the master of the rolls and the lords justices of appeal; and thence to the house of lords.

So much for the ordinary case, turning on ordinary matters of statute and common law. But for the sake of completeness we must note the existence of two other divisions of the high court, besides the queen's bench, the judges of which discharge in the main all the functions so far described. The chancery division exists to try cases arising out of such matters as trusts, wardships, and the disposal of real estate—in short, the kind of suit where the ancient equity jurisdiction of the chancellor was most commonly invoked. As for the probate, divorce, and admiralty division, its functions are as obvious as they are apparently ill-assorted, though the fact that they were both included in the jurisdiction of the ancient church courts provides a link between the first two. The existing church courts, for which the two archbishops appoint a judge, stand quite outside the three divisions and are of little practical importance, except for a very occasional question of ecclesiastical discipline: but they are remarkable in that appeal from them, unlike an appeal from any of the three divisions of the high court, lies to another tribunal than the house of lords.

This is the Judicial Committee of the Privy Council, the more important business of which is the hearing of appeals from all British courts held outside the confines of the United Kingdom and from the courts of those other member states of the Commonwealth which so desire. As regards the law which it may administer, the judicial committee is wholly distinct, for it was willing to take cognizance of Roman–Dutch law from South Africa and old French law from Canada, as well as modern codes of varying origin and native customs from every shore where the British flag may chance to fly. But as regards personnel it is less distinct, for although the judicial committee can call upon the services of a few privy councillors from the judiciary of other parts of the Commonwealth, the nucleus is provided by the nine lords of appeal in ordinary, who are likewise the principal judges in appeals from the courts of the United Kingdom, when they are heard in the house of lords.

3. THE LAW AND THE CITIZEN

The connection between the law and the life of the law-abiding citizen is by no means self-evident. At one time or another he may be involved in some petty case—is prosecuted by the police and pays a small fine, or has a civil action with regard to his business or his home. But when this happens he will entrust his interests to a professional solicitor, who will argue his case for him in any of the lower courts; or, if it is a high court matter, the solicitor will engage a barrister to appear: and the payment of these lawyers' fees rids the citizen of direct responsibility for the conduct of the proceedings. To be arrested and to stand in the dock on a serious criminal charge is the fate of few of us.

Nevertheless, the courts could not function without lay assistance. The holding of assizes and quarter sessions involves the attendance of a large number of jurymen, from whom the juries required to hear particular cases are picked at random. For this purpose any person under 60 years of age is normally liable to serve, provided he is a £20 householder or a freeholder or leaseholder of equivalent financial status: since his presence in court may be needed for several days on end and the maximum compensation payable for loss of earnings is only £1 a day, a shopkeeper or business man may suffer considerable financial loss. The county or borough coroner, the official whose task it is to investigate every death which is not due to obvious natural causes, may also require the help of a smaller jury in determining his verdict. But jury-service devolves automatically and inescapably: a duty which is more tedious and is often shirked is that of giving evidence in courts of law. Most cases which are at all doubtful turn upon the evidence of witnesses, and, if their names are known, they can be compelled to attend court by a writ of subpoena. Otherwise (e.g. in motor accident cases) they often refuse to come forward, partly because of the loss of time involved in what is at best a rather thankless task, and partly from dread of the hostile cross-examination, by means of questions on their evidence, to which they will be submitted by the legal representatives of the other party. The cross-examination system, as a method of finding out the truth, has been described as the glory of the English common law: but it is hardly in the interests of justice that it should also be allowed to operate as a deterrent.

More generally, of course, the machinery of the law, in so far as it runs smoothly, is a protection to the law-abiding citizen. The safeguarding of his person and property against malefactors of all kinds depends not only on the size and efficiency of the police force but also on the fact that the law will usually ensure a speedy conviction, when a criminal is caught. The speedy availability of justice is equally important to the injured party in a civil suit, who in the past was often deterred from appealing to the law by considerations of expense. Since 1949, however, legal advice of all kinds and legal aid in conducting cases both in the county court and in the high court have been made available at little or no charge to any litigant who has neither capital resources nor income in excess of a fixed scale. The same legislation also made it easier than before for poor prisoners to obtain legal aid when standing trial on criminal charges in the higher courts or, in some instances, those held by magistrates. But in all civil disputes the litigant of moderate means remains at a great disadvantage in suing a wealthy person or corporation because, even if he wins, the costs awarded to him are hardly ever the full costs of the action, and if he loses, the costs awarded against him are a far greater burden to him than they would be to his opponent.

The law also protects the citizen, not only against the individual wrong-doer, but against the state. The supreme safeguard of English liberties lies in the fact that the activities of the government, which in many countries are above the law, are here subjected to review in the ordinary law courts. If you are arrested by order of the government or any other authority whatever, you or your friends may apply to a judge for a rule *nisi*, which means that on a named day lawful reason must be given to the judge for your detention (e.g. that you have been lawfully committed to prison to await trial). Failing this, the judge then issues a writ of habeas corpus, which secures your release. Moreover, you will be able to sue the policeman who arrested you, and the courts will not allow the fact that he acted under orders to cover any high-handed conduct. And, more generally, the courts will not allow any official, from the prime minister to the postmaster, to do anything which an ordinary person cannot do, except under statute law or by virtue of some exceptional uses of the royal prerogative, such as that which denies the privileges of habeas corpus to prisoners of war.

Apropos of this, it used to be pointed out that in England there was no such thing as administrative law, or the making of legal decisions by officials. The great increase in the activities of the state during the past half-century has rendered this generalization too sweeping. It is difficult for parliament to find time to discuss the details of bills which necessarily contain a long string of highly technical clauses; and in many matters those technical clauses require frequent modification to meet a changing situation. Therefore the practice has grown up of enacting skeleton legislation, the details of which are to be filled in by the appropriate government department. Such regulations once made are immune from criticism by the courts, because they have been given the force of law beforehand. As long ago as 1909, in a case in which the board of agriculture authorized the compulsory sale of a farm, Mr. Justice Darling found the board to be 'no more impeachable than parliament itself'.

Since 1944 a select committee of the house of commons, normally with a chairman chosen from the opposition, has had the task of scrutinizing all rules and orders issued under any statute which provides for their confirmation or annulment by parliament, so as to call attention to any unusual or undesirable features. But in nine years it commented adversely on less than 2 per cent of some 7,000 orders. Procedure was further tightened up by the passing in 1946 of a statutory instruments act, applicable both to departmental regulations and also to orders in council issued by a department under authority of a statute. They must be published or otherwise made known to those concerned before they can take legal effect; if they require to be laid before parliament in advance of their taking legal effect, any failure to fulfil this requirement must be notified and explained to the lord chancellor and the Speaker; and if they are subject to annulment by resolution of either house, a uniform period of 40 days must be allowed for such action to be taken.

Besides the growth of departmental legislation, serious criticism has been directed to the practice of authorizing officials by statute to decide disputes between their departments and private citizens. Thus, if the ministry of housing and local government decides that a house which you own is unfit for habitation and must be remodelled or demolished, your arguments against this decision are liable to be heard, not in a court of law, but by an inspector of the ministry concerned. If the final decision goes against you and you continue recalcitrant, the courts may be required to issue a writ of Mandamus to compel you to obey the order of the ministry: what the courts may not do is to investigate your case themselves. The members of the tribunal may not have possessed any legal qualification or even the security of tenure needed to make them reasonably unbiased; their decision may have been palpably absurd: but by refusing to publish the reasons on which it is based, they can prevent the courts from intervening even on the grounds that there has been a denial of natural justice.

Some notorious injustices have certainly resulted, which led to the establishment in 1958 of an Advisory Council on Tribunals under the control of the lord chancellor and the secretary of state for Scotland. This body now supervises the membership and procedure of 45 categories of tribunal, with the object of ensuring fairness as between individuals and government departments. But it would be wrong to suppose, for example, that on balance the public interest is not well served by such devices as the local three-man tribunals to which disputes arising out of the administration of the new social services are commonly referred. It is hardly practicable for a government department to disclose every relevant detail of its records and programme. If it did so, litigious individuals might seize the chance to block the way to urgently needed public improvements. Moreover, the law courts have always been accustomed as far as possible to consider the rights of the individual in strict isolation, and will not readily take notice of the wider intentions of parliament. For better and worse, the welfare state requires a different approach if its administrators are to solve their problems to the general benefit, so that the common law courts probably serve the community best, not by replacing administrative courts but by helping to confine them within their proper statutory spheres of action.

VII

THE SERVICE OF THE CROWN

1. THE ARMED FORCES

THE term 'the Services' is restricted in common usage to mean the personnel of the Navy, Army, and Royal Air Force. Historically this is quite reasonable, for England has been defended by a service of professional soldiers and professional sailors since the days of Cromwell and Blake. Some famous regiments were first formed in the reign of Charles II, and the names of our warships—though not a fixed establishment of naval personnel—date back to vessels launched under Tudor auspices. The civil service, by comparison, is extremely new. As late as the eighteenth century the collection of taxes was its only considerable function and government offices in London were manned by a handful of clerks. The number of official employees increased, indeed, with the reforms of the 1830s (e.g. institution of factory inspectors), but it was not until 1870 that the contemptible practice of recruiting mainly among poor relations and dependants of ministers and their parliamentary supporters gave place finally to recruitment by a severe examination. This reform inaugurated the civil service as we know it to-day.

Another reason why we think naturally of the armed forces first is because they seem to concern us more closely. In the distant past it was the armoured knights of William the Conqueror who hammered the mediaeval English kingdom into a shape that it has never wholly lost. In the more recent past it was by force of arms as much as by any other single influence that the empire was built up, from the days of Drake and Ralegh to those of Rhodes, Kitchener, and Lugard. Even now the ordinary citizen is likely to be in more intimate personal contact with the military than with the civil services. He may be attached voluntarily through membership of a cadet force, of the territorial army, or of the army emergency reserve. If his age brings him into the younger categories of the national service regulations, he would continue to be liable to compulsory recall in any emergency up to June 1964. And in case of invasion the common law of the realm has always required the citizen, statute or no statute, to take part in its defence.

Moreover, in Britain as elsewhere the way in which the state controls its armed forces—or in default, is controlled by them—is an important aspect of constitutional development. There have been recent illustrations in various parts of the world, showing that modern weapons make a government and a mass of unarmed citizens, even acting together, helpless if an army or an air force 'pronounces' in favour of some policy of which they disapprove. In England we have enjoyed since 1689 such protection against this as a law can give. Under the mutiny act of that year the maintenance of a standing army in time of peace, declared illegal two months before by the terms of the declaration of rights, was authorized for one year only; and this system of annual authorization is still continued by the army and air force (annual) act. If parliament did not meet one year, or met and refused to pass the act, the continued existence of these forces in any form would involve a breach of statute, and their discipline resting upon military law would become illegal: services in which officers could do no more than sue disobedient subordinates for breach of contract might not be very formidable. A further protection lies in the fact that each of the three services has a civilian minister at its head, who has power to override the decisions of his service advisers on the board of admiralty, army council, or air council. Even at the topmost level, where the four members of the chiefs of staff committee form the equivalent of an inter-service general staff, at least in theory, it is significant that their chairman, who is the effective head for the time being of all the armed forces of the crown, is chief of staff to a civilian minister, the minister of defence, and has as his final arbiter the civilian Defence Committee of the cabinet.

In any threat of civil war the attitude of the army might well prove decisive, witness the alarm in March 1914, when a number of officers stationed at the Curragh, on being questioned (perhaps unwisely) about their intentions in the event of war in Ireland, proposed to resign their commissions or let themselves be cashiered rather than enforce a home rule act against Ulster. It is therefore most important that in any civil disturbance the army should be confined to its primary function of restoring law and order, while the duty of punishment (always liable to be mixed up with politics) is left to the ordinary law courts. Here also we have a most valuable legal principle, the recognition of which goes far to prevent the possibility on English soil of acts of vengeance committed by armies elsewhere in the aftermath of civil war. That principle, enshrined in the petition of right (1628), is the non-recognition of martial law. In actual fighting there is no law, and it may be the duty of soldiers to kill those who resist

The Armed Forces

them, meeting violence with violence. What they are not entitled to do is to employ summary methods for the trial and punishment of prisoners, in relation to whom their only duty is to keep them in safe custody.

A classic illustration of this invaluable rule may be found in the unhappy history of Wolfe Tone, an Irishman who invaded Ireland with a French commission, was captured by the British army, and by it condemned to death.

> On the morning when his execution was about to take place, application was made to the Irish King's Bench for a writ of Habeas Corpus. The Court at once granted the writ. When it is remembered that Wolfe Tone's substantial guilt was admitted, that the Court was made up of judges who detested the rebels, and that in 1798 Ireland was in the midst of a revolutionary crisis, it will be admitted that no more splendid assertion of the supremacy of the law can be found than the protection of Wolfe Tone by the Irish Bench.[1]

At the present day, however, the armed forces of the crown present the citizen with problems of a very different character. Britain is no longer a power of the very first rank, and no efforts on her part can make her so. In the unsettled years of the 1950s as much as 10 per cent of the gross national product was being spent on defence, and 7 per cent of the total working population was absorbed by the Services and the supply of Service needs. Yet the Suez Canal crisis of 1956 revealed that we were no longer in a position to take effective unilateral action to assert our alleged treaty rights, even in regions which had been regarded only a decade before as falling within the sphere of traditional British interests. In addition, the overwhelmingly rapid scientific and technical progress of once

[1] A. V. Dicey: *Law of the Constitution*, p. 290.

backward rivals imposed, as we have indicated, a most severe strain on the national economy to meet a huge defence expenditure, which nevertheless completely failed to produce the sense of security that the Royal Navy had provided so cheaply for so long. Universal disarmament was therefore the policy which would have suited latter-day Britain best, and much earnest propaganda was conducted for the proposal that Britain should lead the way by formally renouncing the manufacture and testing of the hydrogen (megaton) bomb, the weapon of the *guerre à outrance* which might destroy humanity. But to accept one of the alternative assumptions, either that the rest of the world would follow Britain's example; or that the Communist powers would respect her neutrality and refrain from aggression, direct or indirect; or that in the last resort Britain would still be defended by America, seemed to many people to involve too great an act of faith or too little reliance upon the traditional virtue of self-help.

The sequel to the Suez disaster was therefore not any dramatic gesture but a careful scaling-down of British defences, described officially as 'the biggest change in defence policy ever made in normal times'. National service, first instituted in peacetime by the militia act of April 1939, was to be terminated. The Regular Army was to be increased to 375,000 men—almost twice the size of the pre-war army—with a central reserve held in the United Kingdom for rapid movement by air to any theatre of operations. The Royal Navy was to scrap its remaining battleships, including the virgin H.M.S. *Vanguard*, in favour of small striking-forces composed of an aircraft-carrier and guided-missile ships. The Royal Air Force, with a total personnel of 180,000—about three times the pre-war figure—was to provide the chief means both of defence and of retaliation against nuclear attack, pending the use of a ground-to-air guided missile system in defence and of attack on land targets by ballistic rockets launched from ground-level by land or sea.

To some extent the programme outlined in April 1957 has been overtaken by the speed of scientific advance, especially the conquest of outer space. But two basic facts have continued to hold good. One is that the armed forces of the British crown, after some two and a half centuries of cumulatively great achievement, can no longer attempt to measure up to the forces of the two world powers, either in any general deployment of strength or even in the exercise of control over a limited region, such as a disputed colonial territory. The other is that there can no longer be any guaranteed defence of England itself, which Shakespeare saw as

> hedged in with the main,
> That water-walled bulwark, still secure
> And confident from foreign purposes.

'Foreign purposes' overshadow the lives of Queen Elizabeth II's subjects with a persistence unknown even in Armada days. For, in the measured language of a government White Paper:

> It must be frankly recognized that there is at present no means of providing adequate protection for the people of this country against the consequences of an attack with nuclear weapons ... The overriding consideration in all military planning must be to prevent war rather than to prepare for it.[1]

[1] Para. 12 of *Defence. Outline of Future Policy.* Cmd. 124.

2. THE CIVIL SERVICE

The term 'civil service' covers, in theory, all non-military permanent servants of the state—the ubiquitous postman, for example—but the hub of the whole system is the group of public offices in or near Whitehall, where the more important functionaries for the most part do their work. Their activities lack the glamour of the military career, and it is possible to disparage 'Whitehall' as a place where everything is done in an endless routine of documents neatly tied together with the famous red tape; though any large office, public or private, would in fact fall into confusion without the routine. Moreover, in the case of a government office there are additional strong reasons for recording every decision and taking special care to follow precedent. Civil servants are expected by the public to show strict impartiality in their dealings; and when they fail in this or any other important aspect of their duties responsibility for the failure has to be accepted in parliament by a minister, who may even be driven to resign as a result of some reckless action on the part of a subordinate official.

Lord Balfour describes the position of civil servants as follows:

> They do not control policy: they are not responsible for it. Belonging to no party, they are for that very reason an invaluable element in Party Government. It is through them, especially through their higher branches, that the transference of responsibility from one party or one minister to another involves no destructive shock to the administrative machine. There may be change of direction, but the curve is smooth.[1]

[1] Earl of Balfour: Introduction to Bagehot's *English Constitution*, p. xxiv.

Thus the cabinet decides what general policy it will pursue—whether to allocate larger sums of public money to the work of any particular department or to economize, whether to increase its sphere of action by new legislation or to let well alone—but the actual functioning of the department is the concern of the officials and depends primarily upon their traditions and energy. Moreover, the cabinet also relies mainly upon the civil service for the accumulation and sifting of the information upon which new policies must initially be based.

Such responsible work requires first-rate men. Civil service commissioners were appointed in 1855 to organize admission by examination, and since 1870 this has been fixed by order in council as the regular method of entry. The tests are competitive, but broadly speaking the standard for the administrative class is that of a university graduate with high honours, for the executive class that of an above-average sixth form school-leaver; there is also promotion from grade to grade within the service. There are not more than 5,000 administrative civil servants, the men (and a few women) who take important decisions and help to shape the policy of their department. For each of them there are about 12 executive officers, who conduct the detailed business within a prescribed framework, and about 60 clerks and typists. Less easy to fit into the scheme of things is the increasing body of professional, scientific, and technical advisers, who have to be specially recruited to meet present-day needs: even in departments with a strongly technical basis they as yet rarely reach posts at the top to correspond, say, with those of generals serving on the army council. But it is clear that the administrative grade at least has great opportunities to offer—for the very best the headship of a department, which may mean more power behind the scenes than is exercised by the minister himself in front; for many others the eventual charge of an important division or branch or perhaps of a regional headquarters of a ministry, some degree of decentralization having become fairly common since the war.

Civil servants suffer one important disability. Since they must serve with equal loyalty whatever political party may be in office, it would not do for them to be strong party men. Since secret or at least confidential transactions must pass before the eyes of even the humbler ranks, their participation in public controversy must always involve a risk of indiscretion or worse. Accordingly, from the typing and clerical grades upwards civil servants are forbidden to play any active part in politics, though they of course retain the vote; even to stand for a local council requires permission from the head of the department. In other respects their position is in practice a good one—reasonably well paid and dignified, with security of tenure and a generous pension. In legal theory, however, there are serious disabilities which apply to all civil servants as employees of the crown. They have no remedy against their dismissal, however arbitrary, and no means of enforcing payment of their pensions: for it is a principle of English law that the crown cannot hamper its own future actions, because it must be free to act for the public good. At the same time, no case will lie against the head of the department or whoever else made the engagement that has been broken, because all civil servants are equally in the service of the crown and cannot be regarded as employers one of another. Until 1948 there were other disadvantages that resulted from the ancient maxim that the king can do no wrong, the employee of the crown being in principle solely answerable for civil wrongs committed in the course of his employment, though there was a cumbrous procedure made available at the attorney-general's discretion called a petition of right. But at the present day the crown can be sued as easily as any other employer in such cases, except as regards unregistered postal packets, telephonic communications, and acts of the armed forces while on duty. However, the law which prescribes these exceptions also exempts from personal liability the civil servant or member of the armed forces concerned.

The important departments of state are now about thirty in number, of which some are financial (the treasury, ministry of pensions and national insurance, etc.), some concerned with external relations (foreign office, commonwealth relations office, or the ministries concerned with defence), and others with the internal administration of the country (the home office, for example, and most of the newer ministries, such as those of health, labour, and transport). If the political head is a secretary of state, the civil service head of the department is styled the permanent under-secretary of state; otherwise the civil service head who acts directly under the minister is known as the permanent secretary. His chief subordinates will include one or more deputy secretaries, several under-secretaries, and assistant secretaries. Since the departments broadly resemble each other in organization, we may turn to a brief description of the activities of two or three of particular interest and importance.

The civil service head of the foreign office has long been a personage of great influence, whose views on current affairs—to say nothing of his past recommendations, enshrined in state papers—have sometimes been allowed to interest the public as much as those of a minister. The staff under him are divided into departments, each of which specializes in relations with a particular region: they will normally have spent a part of their time in the embassies and consulates abroad, the staff of which constitutes the Foreign Service and is administered by the foreign office. Dispatches and other speedier modern types of communication pass to and fro, enabling the foreign office to formulate its proposals as minutes, which combine information regarding a current situation with recommendations for future action. State papers of this kind may originate with quite junior officials and pass through many hands, until they are finally transmitted by the under-secretary to the secretary of state for the consideration of the cabinet.

The chief concerns of the home office are defined by *Whitaker's Almanack* as—

> the maintenance of law and order; the efficiency of the police service; the treatment of offenders, including juvenile offenders; the efficiency of the Probation Service; the organization of Magistrates' Courts; legislation on criminal justice; the supervision of the Fire Service; the preparations for Civil Defence Services; the care of children by local authorities and voluntary societies; the regulation of the employment of children and young persons; the control and naturalization of aliens; the law relating to parliamentary and local government elections.

Thirteen other 'miscellaneous subjects' are also listed, and a good deal of formal work is involved in the fact that the home secretary is the channel of communication between the queen and her subjects. Although it is the exercise of the royal prerogative of pardon which chiefly focuses public attention on this department from time to time, a far more significant continuous activity is the enforcement of rules which (as we can see) widely affect both public and private life. For this purpose the home office employs some five or six distinct bodies of highly qualified inspectors.

The treasury is the only department which has joint permanent secretaries. One of these combines his treasury post with that of secretary to the cabinet, and his wide general control of affairs is further exemplified by the title of Head of Her Majesty's Home Civil Service. The other handles chiefly questions of economic policy, with which the state is nowadays closely concerned, and he works with an economic section of civil servants and an economic planning board of eminent advisers. The board was set up in 1947 to advise on the best use of the economic resources of the United Kingdom: the much more recent division of the secretary's responsibilities may be taken to mark a permanent acceptance of these new functions by the state. But it has long been the business of treasury officials to estimate and approve the cost of any act of policy pursued at the public expense. For instance, they prepare all the data for the budget which their political head, the chancellor of the exchequer, presents year by year to the house of commons. Three consequences follow from this. Firstly, as all officials receive their salaries from the public purse, it is the treasury that regulates the conditions under which the officials in all the departments serve: it has the whip-hand of them. Secondly, as most legislation involves expenditure of some kind, the treasury has the right to examine all legislative proposals drafted by other departments. And, as if that were not power enough, the importance of the financial aspect of any course of action has led to the growth of a practice by which even a mere proposal involving expenditure is not considered by the cabinet—the supreme organ of government—unless it has been fully examined beforehand by the treasury, in concert with the department concerned. Thus the treasury rather than the house of commons is nowadays the guardian of the public purse.

3. PAYING FOR IT

Some of the lesser government departments commonly engage in remunerative projects—the ministry of works reconditions historic buildings and charges a fee for admission; the forestry commission has over a million acres under plantation; and the ordnance survey is not alone in making a substantial profit on its publications. Long before the days of nationalized industries there were certain public utility services, of which the Port of London Authority (1908) was the oldest and the BBC the best known, that were designed to recover their costs by sale of services. Most notable example of all, there is the Post Office, which claims to have been one of the great revenue-collecting departments from its inception in 1660, while developing a whole series of invaluable facilities for the public convenience, including not only the royal mails but telegraph and telephone services and inexpensive means both for transmitting money and for saving it.

But from this point of view departments fall into two main divisions. The home and foreign offices are examples of a type that is predominantly engaged in tasks of administration and advice. Others, including those concerned with defence and the social services, which we shall be considering in later chapters, are directly engaged in providing for the public needs. The former type requires only to pay its staff, the latter must be furnished with very much larger sums to pay for the services themselves. Accordingly, the general problem of public expenditure is one of great size and intricacy.

Orthodox financiers of the Gladstonian era used to maintain that taxation should be half direct and half indirect, because direct taxes are paid mostly in proportion to wealth, so that a few rich people contribute more than many poor; whereas indirect taxes levied upon the cost of commodities fall equally heavily upon all users of the commodity taxed, which may be such a thing as tea or sugar, of which a comparatively poor family uses nearly as much as a rich one. In any case taxation is more onerous for the poor man, since in order to pay even a little he may have to go without something he really needs, while the rich man, however much he pays, is thereby being deprived of luxuries rather than necessities. But if the poor paid no taxes whatever, so the orthodox argued, they would vote without reserve in favour of the most lavish public expenditure.

Indirect taxes—which produce considerably less than half the national income now—are mostly collected by the board of customs and excise, employing a large staff of executive civil servants. They are familiar to many of us at the ports, where foreign goods except most raw materials are compelled to pay import duties or customs. Excise means the levying of similar duties upon certain commodities, not at the ports (for most of them are made at home) but when they come to be used by the public. Beer and tobacco are the big traditional examples, but the entertainments duty introduced after the first world war followed the same plan of taxing luxuries which are nevertheless used by poor as well as rich. There is also a heavy tax on petrol (about one-half the total cost), which not only affects motor-owners directly but is passed on to millions of others in the increased cost of a taxi-ride or the delivery of a parcel. Another form of taxation, which is levied in a sense directly though not as a percentage on income, is the licence or stamp duty, which has to be paid (usually by a simple post office transaction) in order to keep a dog or a gun, place a motor vehicle upon the road, or give validity to many types of legal document.

But direct taxation, properly speaking, is the concern of another very large government department, the board of inland revenue, with its staff of inspectors and collectors scattered all over the country. Under the system of PAYE, which was introduced during the second world war, when income tax first reached the mass of weekly wage-earners, tax is deducted by the employer before paying the employee. Even so, it remains an extremely complicated and burdensome task to extract a due proportion of income, subject to family and numerous other allowances and at a rate which may vary with each annual budget, from the separate incomes of approximately one-quarter of the entire population. If the income exceeds £5,000 a year there will be surtax to be paid in addition; and any property or capital of a value of more than £3,000 pays estate duty whenever the owner dies. This duty, levied according to a steeply graduated scale, takes at least two-thirds of what a millionaire bequeaths to his heirs and, where land is concerned, may make it necessary for a whole estate to be broken up in order to find the money.

Both revenue departments pay their receipts daily into the government account at the Bank of England, known as the consolidated fund, from which nearly all payments for government expenditure are made. The inflow and outflow do not, of course, invariably correspond, but the government—which in financial matters means chiefly the all-powerful officials of the treasury—have several methods of raising temporary loans in the City, quite apart from the large-scale permanent loans, which parliament authorizes (especially in time of war) and which constitute the national debt proper. But for our purpose it is important to remember that a large part of the taxation is returned directly to a section of the community (though not to that section which pays most taxes) in the form of social services.

Although this is a trend which only began in the present century, on the eve of the second world war social services were already costing the state as much as the service of the national debt and the upkeep of the armed forces put together. Since that time both the latter items have undergone a tremendous increase, but the central government services (to be examined in the next chapter) are nevertheless the principal object to which the modern state deliberately diverts the money that in Gladstone's day was left to 'fructify in the pocket of the tax-payer'.

VIII

SOME CENTRAL SERVICES

1. SOCIAL INSURANCE AND SOCIAL ASSISTANCE

THESE terms would have seemed almost meaningless in reference to the functions of the state only a generation or two ago. Originally its accepted functions were virtually restricted to two—the conduct of external relations and the maintenance of the king's peace. Out of the latter there grew in the time of Elizabeth I a system of poor relief, which for two and a half centuries stood alone as a publicly provided amelioration for the life of the masses. The late eighteenth and nineteenth centuries witnessed a considerable extension of local services, necessitated by the growth of town life, but apart from the central control of the workhouses by the poor law board (expanded into the local government board in 1871), the only important national service was the provision of primary education on a local basis under state supervision by the 1870 education act. The public elementary school was available for all but was designed, like the poor law institution, to meet the minimum needs of a single class.

The Liberal governments of 1905–15 were responsible for two important changes. The duty of the state to minister to the poor was for the first time treated as something more than a regrettable necessity. The introduction of non-contributory old age pensions was an important new departure, although the amount (paid through the post office) was only 5s. a week at 70, reduced to 7s. 6d. for a married couple and to nothing for anybody with an existing income of 10s. Important, too, was the meals service instituted at some elementary schools, though it was restricted to those 'unable by reason of lack of food to take full advantage of the education provided for them'. For this was *social assistance* rendered outside the poor law with its stigma to some part of the two age groups that are least able to take care of themselves. Then in 1911 Lloyd George's insurance act carried the activities of the state into much wider fields. Free doctoring and sickness allowances were provided, in return for an insurance payment of 4d. a week by each employee, for virtually the entire wage-earning population. By the same act employees in certain industries, notably ship-building and engineering, which were specially liable to seasonal fluctuations, paid $2\frac{1}{2}d$. a week to receive unemployment pay for a maximum period of fifteen weeks a year. Since comparable payments were also required from employers, the liability incurred by the state was small: but this was the modest beginning of the great edifice of *social insurance*.

Between 1914 and 1939 these services were considerably extended. The biggest developments were the subsidized local housing schemes (see p. 153). But the abolition of the old poor law in 1929 meant that social assistance became more systematically and humanely administered by the local authorities, into whose hands it now passed. A few years later an attempt was made to regularize arrangements for the relief of long-term unemployment, which insurance could not cover, by the introduction of a central Unemployment Assistance Board to control relief paid from central funds. Insurance was likewise extended during the inter-war period, firstly, to cover nearly all wage-earners against temporary unemployment, and secondly, to provide pensions for the widows and orphans of insured persons. Nevertheless, it cannot be pretended that the services proved adequate to the needs of the 1930s, when unemployment rose to a peak approaching 3,750,000 (insured and uninsured) early in 1933 and never fell appreciably below the 2,000,000 mark. For there were a number of bitterly distressed regions—Special Areas, in the official terminology of the day—such as the Welsh coal valleys, Newcastle and county Durham, and Clydeside, where mass unemployment persisted year after year and the standard of living was allowed to fall to a shamefully low minimum.

The memory of this was one big factor in the political revolution of 1945, when the Labour party obtained not merely its first majority at the polls but a majority of nearly 200 seats. But there were three other factors that also prepared the way for the big changes of 1946–50. Extensive new services had been established on a temporary basis to meet the wartime emergencies of bombing, evacuation and dispersal of families, and redistribution of labour. Government expenditure during the war suggested that there was no financial limit to what the state could undertake. Last but not least, there was the key role that had been played in our wartime propaganda by the vision of the future presented in (lord) Beveridge's *Report on Social Insurance and the Allied Services*, an official document of 1942.

The post-war policy, which came to be accepted by all political parties, is based upon the assumption that the first charge upon the national income should be the provision of a minimum standard of life for all at a level which an awakened national conscience can find acceptable. Therefore the new National Assistance Board was 'designed to complete the break-up of the Poor Law' by giving it wide powers to help all persons in need, which in an emergency may include even persons in full-time employment. In addition, three large categories of the population —children and 'youth', the old, and the physically and mentally handicapped—were singled out by special legislation to have more than their barest needs covered at the public expense.

At the same time the call upon social assistance was reduced by the extension of social insurance to virtually the entire population as a safeguard against most of the hazards that can threaten the standard of life. Protection is now provided against the draining away of all personal resources through sickness or industrial injury; unemployment; retirement; maternity and burial expenses; or the death of a wage-earner having a dependent family. The insurance system, however, leaves many hard cases, for which assistance provides a supplementary resource. In addition, two forms of help from public funds were instituted without any reference either to insurance or to any presumptive need for assistance. In 1945 family allowances were enacted, to be paid for all except the eldest child; and the housing act of 1949 repealed all restrictions upon the class of occupant for whom local authorities were allowed to provide subsidized accommodation.

Space will not permit us to study more than one service in detail. But the general picture of growth can be seen partly in terms of money spent: in 1913–14, for example, the civil estimates for education, science, and art amounted to less than £20,000,000; in 1957–8 the corresponding figure was about £430,000,000—an enormous increase even after allowing for the fall in purchasing power. It can also be stated as a whole in terms of the growth of civil service departments concerned. Before the first world war these were broadly speaking three in number—board of education, local government board, and national health insurance commissions—and their non-industrial staff totalled just over 4,000. Ten years after the second war we find twice as many departments are involved—four ministries, the national assistance board, and the children's department of the home office—and the corresponding staff totalled nearly 60,000.

2. THE NATIONAL HEALTH SERVICE

Established after much conflict with vested interests in 1948, a monument to the political skill and determination of the late Aneurin Bevan, the health service would in any case deserve special consideration as the outstanding achievement of British social planning. It is a convenient example, too, because the ministry of health, set up in 1919 with duties which included supervision of local government and housing, has now become a department devoted almost entirely to administering the new service. The example is, however, also characteristic in several respects of the so-called English genius for compromise: thus the health of the school-child remains the separate responsibility of the school medical service, which was established under the then board of education in 1907, while that of the worker at his place of employment is left to private enterprise as regards the fulfilment of specific health and safety requirements laid down by law.

The National Health Service

The ministry has the help of an advisory health services council, composed mainly of professional experts, whose annual report must be laid before parliament. There are also nine standing advisory committees to deal with technical aspects of the work, such as tuberculosis precautions or cancer and radiography. This is the more important, as two of the three main aspects of the ministry's activities bring it into close relations with highly organized professional interests having a strong scientific basis.

The first of these activities is the hospital service, with which the work of medical specialists and particularly of surgeons is directly linked. It employs nearly half a million people, which makes it the third largest national organization, and the service is scattered all over the country in units of very varying size, tradition, and equipment. Exceptional importance attaches to the 36 teaching hospitals, where eminent specialists provide the practical instruction for students, without which the medical profession could not be properly educated: they are allowed their own boards of governors directly responsible to the ministry. These and many less famous hospitals were established, mainly in the eighteenth and nineteenth centuries, by voluntary enterprise upon whatever basis their founders thought conducive to the welfare of their particular localities. A large number of general and special hospitals, cottage hospitals, and sanatoria had also been directly provided by local authorities in more recent years, while another group of about 500 inherited the grim traditions of the old poor law infirmaries.

A central department could not hope to control so complicated a network directly, although the financing under the new system was to be a central government responsibility. To give local authorities charge of hospitals, when they were not rate-supported institutions, would have had several disadvantages, including difficulties with the medical profession. Accordingly, the essential link between the ministry of health and the public which uses the hospitals has taken the form of a system of nominated, unpaid boards and committees. England and Wales were divided into 14 hospital regions, each of which has a board of members nominated by the ministry who are empowered to make all major decisions for their region. The regional board in its turn appoints and supervises the work done by the members of local hospital management committees, each of which is responsible for the day-to-day running of the hospital service in its neighbourhood.

The second main task is the provision of an adequate number of personal practitioners—a name used to embrace family doctors, dentists, pharmacists, and opticians. Regard had to be taken to the distaste with which most doctors received any suggestion that they should become salaried state officials: the need for effective supervision had somehow to be adjusted to the desire for an untrammelled relationship between doctor and patient. Patients were therefore left free to select their doctor, and doctors were left free to accept such patients—up to a prescribed maximum list—as they themselves preferred. In each county or county borough the quality of the medical service provided in this way was to be controlled by a local executive council of 25 members, 12 being appointed by the practitioners themselves, eight by the local authority, and five by the ministry. Under this system it has been necessary to offer special financial incentives to try to increase the supply of doctors in some of the socially least attractive areas.

The third function of the national health service comprises preventive activities, including the whole range of maternity and child welfare services; vaccination and measures against tuberculosis; and all provision made for the aged except in hospitals. These, together with the ambulance service, are administered by local authorities, subject to some supervision by a division of the ministry—the only part of the health service over which the elected representatives of the people have full control.

3. THE SCIENTIFIC CIVIL SERVICE

The growth of the welfare state has been accompanied in a sense by that of the scientific state: for in recent years the needs of defence, trade interests, and social progress have combined to drive the state or its emissaries into the field of invention, where private enterprise long reigned supreme. Even military and naval inventions used to be developed very largely by private contractors, though the royal ordnance factories and the department of the director of naval construction played a distinguished role. Economic difficulties experienced in the first world war produced as early as 1915

> a strong consensus of opinion among persons engaged both in science and in industry that a special need exists at the present time for new machinery and for additional State assistance in order to promote and organize scientific research with a view especially to its application to trade and industry . . . It appears incontrovertible that if we are to advance or even maintain our industrial position we must as a nation aim at such a development of scientific and industrial

research as will place us in a position to . . . compete successfully with the most highly organized of our rivals.[1]

Such research was accordingly entrusted to a committee of the privy council, consisting of the lord president, five other members of the cabinet, and three ex-ministers, including lord Haldane. With the help of an advisory council of scientists and industrialists, by December 1916 a regular civil service organization had been formed—the Department for Scientific and Industrial Research.

The new department became in the course of time the founder and originator of several research establishments, each with its own consultative council and a staff of scientific officers ranking as civil servants: one of these was the so-called 'directorate of tube alloys', set up in September 1941 to further the production of the atomic bomb. So convenient an arrangement led also to the inclusion of various existing research establishments under the aegis of the committee of the privy council and the DSIR. The most important of these and the dates at which they were included are as follows: the National Physical Laboratory (1918), the Geological Survey (1919), Road Research (1933), and Building Research (1950). Finally, in 1956 the main advisory council was found not unreasonably to be overloaded with unpaid responsibilities, and was replaced by an executive research council for the supervision of all research programmes undertaken by authority of the committee of the privy council.

The committee of council has rarely if ever met as a committee, but the ministers who belong to it have taken a natural interest in such researches at least as concerned

[1] *Scheme for the Organization and Development of Scientific and Industrial Research*, Cd. 8005.

their respective ministries. As chairman of the committee the lord president is answerable to cabinet and parliament for the money expended, in 1960–1 a sum of nearly £13,000,000: but his connection with the work itself is sufficiently remote to preserve freedom of enquiry for the scientists. Such a convenient form of organization has tended to spread. Thus a committee of the privy council for medical research took over activities originally associated with Lloyd George's health insurance scheme: it operates through an executive research council, composed mainly of medical men. Agricultural research has been similarly reorganized, and finally in 1956 another committee of council was placed in charge of the Nature Conservancy, which administers some 60 nature reserves and their research stations.

Other departments, particularly those concerned with defence, have inevitably made increasing use of scientists. In 1956 the number of scientific civil servants employed by DSIR was 2,237: this was roughly equal to the number employed by the other civil departments taken together, but four times as many had employment with the defence departments (including the ministry of supply). Moreover, in 1954 a new scientific department was created by parliament, the United Kingdom Atomic Energy Authority, which was to combine fundamental research and the production of fissile material with the study of industrial applications and the production of atomic weapons for the ministry of supply. To achieve results in these fields it was considered desirable to try to combine strict government control with the freedom and flexibility of a privately run industry. The method adopted was to constitute as the Authority a body consisting of a chairman and four full-time members, which was originally linked with the cabinet and parliament through the lord president of the council, but latterly this link with key scientists has been maintained by the prime minister in person; at the end of the decade its expenditure was about £100,000,000 a year.

4. NATIONALIZED INDUSTRIES

In the long run the scientific services may have greater effects upon the lives of us all, but the nationalized industries are the sphere in which the day-to-day impact of new state services is most insistent. Although the policy of nationalization of industry is associated primarily with the Labour government of 1945-51, their actions had some earlier precedents. Both the railways and the coal-mines had been administered by the government during the first world war. The royalties paid to landowners by the coal-mines were nationalized in 1938. Under the threat of invasion in 1940 parliament placed all private property at the disposal of the state, and throughout the following five years private enterprise was completely overshadowed by the gigantic state-organized demands of the war effort. Structurally, however, the most interesting precedent was the public utility trust, where a monopoly was set up by law to arrange for the efficient independent management of a concern of special public importance.

The earliest was the Port of London Authority, planned by Lloyd George in 1908, which together with the London Passenger Transport Board of 1933 will be dealt with as a metropolitan institution (p. 162). In both these cases, as we shall see, the management was not directly linked with the government. But when the British Broadcasting Corporation was established to operate the radio monopoly in December 1926 the fact that its revenue was collected for it in licences issued by the state, and still more the importance of its news services in an emergency (as had been shown during the general strike the previous May), argued for a closer relationship. The posts of the chairman and governors, who were responsible through the director-general for the staff, the programmes, and the technical efficiency of the service, were therefore made crown appointments for short terms of years, filled by the prime minister on the recommendation of the postmaster-general. Thus the policy though not the day-to-day working of the BBC was recognized to be a national concern, for which the postmaster-general was answerable to parliament; the charter itself was also granted subject to decennial renewal. The same kind of responsibility was required of the Central Electricity Board, an exact contemporary of the BBC, which was formed to erect the grid for a nation-wide distribution of electric power, and the British Overseas Airways Corporation, which when war broke out was in process of formation to replace two subsidized private companies in the development of civil aviation. The members of the board were to be appointed by the minister of transport, those of the corporation by the minister for air.

The Labour government after the war proposed to carry out a programme of long standing, which aimed at the socialization of the main instruments of production. The Bank of England, the coal-mines, gas and electricity undertakings, transport, and iron and steel were then all to be nationalized, but most of the road haulage and the iron and steel industry were subsequently returned to private hands. The change made little apparent difference to the bank, which for many years had worked in the closest co-operation with the treasury. Both gas and electricity had been supplied over a long period by many local government authorities, and the wholesale distribution of electricity was already, as we have seen, a state concern. But state ownership of the coal-mines and transport undertakings involved the organization of public control over the two largest groups of employees in the country. Moreover, control would have to reconcile three divergent interests—the high expectations of the workers, the needs of the consumers, and the concern of the government with viability, having regard to the capital sums invested in each industry, for which compensation was now to be paid from government funds. Were the workers to become industrial civil servants, like the technical staff of the post office? Was a minister to be answerable to parliament for the day-to-day conduct of business? If not, how was parliament to ensure a reasonable degree of efficiency in the conduct of enterprises with such huge ramifications?

The method adopted was to establish a board or commission to operate each of the new services, working under the ultimate authority of a minister but relieving him of any direct responsibility for detailed matters of administration. This makes it possible to keep the ministries of power and transport and civil aviation of reasonable size. It prevents time-consuming discussion in parliament of detailed matters of business management on which it is often ill-qualified to pass judgment. Most important of all, it leaves the staff of each nationalized industry with some chance of developing the qualities of elasticity and initiative needed to keep abreast of technical progress, especially where they are burdened with much obsolete equipment. Members are nominated by the minister concerned: in each case there is a chairman with one or more deputies and a combination of full- and part-time members, making a total of not more than a dozen. The British Transport Commission at first delegated powers of administration and development to a series of Executives, dealing with separate branches. In 1953 the commission was reconstituted on the basis of a single centralized control, but in 1961 the government was preparing to abolish the commission, leaving only a National Transport Advisory Council: power would then be exercised by five separate boards for railways, docks, inland waterways, London transport, and other activities.

The regional structure is of great importance. The coal board and transport commission compose their regional boards of nominated members, but on the railways it was planned in 1961 to substitute regional boards with virtual autonomy. There are nine divisional boards for coal; the members other than the chairman and his deputy are allocated respectively to finance, production, labour, and marketing, the main managerial units being smaller areas within the divisions, for no two coal-mines have exactly the same problems to face. The Central Electricity Generating Board likewise governs its local divisions, but the Electricity and Gas Councils, of which the latter is formed of area board chairmen, do not govern the regional organizations. In both these cases the members of area boards are direct nominees of the ministry, who manage the business through a number of sub-areas as public corporations in their own right. Each area board is linked up with local consumer interests through a consultative council nominated by the ministry, a majority of whose members are designated by local authorities.

Nevertheless, it remained an open question whether a greater degree of decentralization or some method of giving increased responsibility to the rank and file of workers or a more generous attitude to the financing side was what was still lacking to enable nationalization to function with complete efficiency. The experience of the first decade and a half did not lead to any widespread demand for its immediate extension into other fields.

IX

LOCAL GOVERNMENT

1. HISTORICAL

THE most ancient subdivisions of the country—indeed, they are not really subdivisions at all, for they existed long before national unity was achieved—are the shire and the township. From the shire we get the modern county, and there are many people who still feel a genuine county patriotism, not least in the cricket season. For this is a unit which has never lost reality. The first kings of all England made the county court, over which the sheriff presided, their chief instrument of local administration. The early Norman kings likewise used it for military, fiscal, and judicial purposes, and when parliaments began it was in the county court that the knights of the shire were elected. Thereafter it fell into disrepute, but by the Tudor era the powers of local government had been transferred to a new county organization, namely the justices of the peace meeting in quarter sessions, whom innumerable statutes empowered to levy local taxes and minister to every local need, from the keeping up of bridges to the keeping down of alehouses. This autocratic system of county administration was to last four centuries.

The name of 'township', on the other hand, in its original application to the Anglo-Saxon village, has long ceased to be used—except, perhaps, on antiquated boundary stones. With the coming of Christianity it was supplemented by the term 'parish', for the area to which one priest and one church ministered commonly coincided with the township. Feudalism, again, introduced a third unit, the manor with its dues and obligations, which likewise tended to conform with pre-existing limits of area. Nevertheless, the village as it re-emerged into the light of (Tudor) day was largely self-governing in form. Either the manor court survived, in which the tenants of the manor declared what ought to be done in local affairs, or, more usually, the business was transacted by a parish Vestry, a meeting of all adult male inhabitants which took its name from the natural place of assembly. Here the local officials, notably the constable and the overseers of the poor, were elected year by year, and their names laboriously inscribed in the church registers.

Meanwhile, towns in the modern sense were springing up—centres of trade and industry where a more progressive population developed strong common interests and a desire to free themselves from outside interference. This could be achieved by means of a charter or series of charters, paid for usually in the hard cash with which trading centres would be comparatively well supplied. From the lord of the manor they would buy immunity from his exactions of feudal dues; from the king—more important —they would buy all kinds of privileges, ranging between the holding of a market or fair and the power of trying lawsuits and collecting taxes without the interference of his officers. These charters varied immensely, but a common feature of chartered boroughs was the establishment of their own ruling body or corporation, which in the course of time often became a narrow oligarchy entirely lacking in public spirit. Such were the corporations that corruptly sold the representation of boroughs in eighteenth-century parliaments.

Reform came in two ways. From about 1750 it was usual for centres of population, especially new ones such as Manchester or Birmingham, to ask parliament to pass private acts setting up a local committee for such purposes as lighting, cleansing, or policing the streets, duties which the existing local authority could not or would not carry out. These special Statutory Authorities became very numerous, and provided the pattern for a type of general reform (i.e. reforms enacted for the whole country) that began with the new poor law of 1834. Since the reign of Elizabeth I poor relief had been administered by the overseers and at the expense of each parish, subject to the supervision of quarter sessions. To tighten up the system and reduce expenditure the act of 1834 established boards of guardians elected by the ratepayers, who administered relief under the auspices of a new government authority. The boards, however, were not given control of a single parish, but of a specially created subdivision of the county, known as the poor law union. During the ensuing forty years this method was extensively followed, until England had been carved up into highway, burial, sanitary, and school board districts, each of which, like the poor law union, acted for an area of separately defined boundaries.

The reason may have been that parliament was at bottom reluctant to give large powers to any one subordinate authority. This is borne out by the rather grudging way in which the other and more sweeping type of reform was inaugurated. The municipal corporations act of 1835 did make an immense change by providing the uniform, democratic system of borough government which still obtains; but apart from elementary powers of police, lighting, and sanitation, the functions of a modern municipality were all conferred step by step by much later legislation. Moreover, it was not until 1888 that the still more undemocratic though less corrupt system of county government was likewise swept away, when the administrative powers of the justices at quarter sessions, enumerated under sixteen heads, were likewise transferred to a democratically elected county council, the form of which remains substantially unaltered to-day. By the same act the larger towns were given a more independent status under the new name of county boroughs.

The last big change of organization came in 1894 and had two distinct aspects. The county, the size of which commonly renders it an unwieldy unit of administration, was subdivided into urban and rural districts, each with its council performing certain restricted functions (including the collection of the rates) under the county council's supervision, and the rural district was to be further subdivided for small matters under parish councils. At the same time a start was made in the long process of abolishing other specially created subdivisions, sanitary boards, for instance, being merged in the new creations. School board districts followed suit in 1902, and in 1929 the abolition of boards of guardians completed the important process of concentrating powers of local self-government in the hands of a few fully representative bodies, which now administer practically all statutes dealing with local affairs.

In 1957–8, however, two royal commissions were set up to make a comprehensive review of local government organization, with special regard to the complexity of existing arrangements in the greater London area and in five other big conurbations. Their task was expected to occupy six years in all and to rouse some controversy. This duly began when the first commission reported with unexpected speed and unanimity in favour of a new two-tier authority—a Council of Greater London elevated above the councils of enlarged London boroughs. Opposition was also likely to be strong to some of the second commission's proposals for the provinces: one county (Rutland) was to be completely abolished, and in the Black Country the new 'pattern of five county boroughs' entirely eliminated 17 existing units.

2. THE LOCAL COUNCILS OF TO-DAY

As regards the geographical area over which it holds sway, the largest local authority is undoubtedly the council of a rural county, such as Devonshire. We specify 'rural' because industrial areas inside the county are to a large extent withdrawn from the direct control of the county council. Nevertheless, we shall leave the county council to be discussed later for two reasons: rural England has, on the average, a rather less vigorous political life, and the work of the councils is therefore not quite so interesting; and the United Kingdom is predominantly a land of town dwellers.

The form of government prevailing in a town may belong to any of three types, and the size of its population will mainly determine which. If it has more than 50,000 inhabitants it will probably be a county borough, which means that the borough council is entirely immune from the intervention of the council of the county in which the borough happens to be situated: such a borough constitutes an administrative county of its own. More than eighty of these county boroughs having been established since 1888, admission to the rank has not latterly been conceded to towns with a population of less than 100,000, and in view of the royal commissions no further individual applications will be allowed until 1973. Next there is the municipal borough, a category into which any large market town, if it is ancient or has a population of more than 20,000 (and less than 50,000), may be expected to fall. Municipal boroughs are of several different types—some are called cities, which usually betokens the seat of a bishop; many, but not all, have their separate quarter sessions and recorder; and the smallest, places like the ancient cinque port towns of Romney and Rye, are usually content with the minimum of municipal activity that will enable them to retain their special status. But all municipal boroughs have two features in common, one of which is their form of government—the town council—and the other their dependence in some degree upon the county council. All municipal boroughs elect county councillors, but the services rendered by the county council tend to vary inversely with the population, though since 1930 even the larger boroughs have been deprived successively of control of their poor relief, education, police, and health services.

Lastly, a town that represents a new growth of population or which is small though ancient and was never chartered as a borough in its early days, may be governed by an urban district council. If so, it will differ from a municipal borough chiefly in dignity, for it will have no mayor and aldermen, only councillors; the difference in legal powers and functions is now small. Nevertheless, an urban district still commonly aspires to extend its boundaries, increase its population, and petition the crown for incorporation as a borough.

Municipal boroughs, which are about four times as numerous as county boroughs, likewise have their aspirations to higher rank. One or two of the oldest have populations of less than 2,000, while several of those most recently incorporated in the outer London area exceed 200,000. But as regards the general system all boroughs are sufficiently similar to be grouped together. All parliamentary voters are entitled to vote in council elections, held in each ward—the electoral divisions of the town—annually; but each ward normally has three representatives on the council, who sit for three years, so that the annual contest is for the return of one member only. These councillors, however, do not constitute the whole council, for ever since 1835 the law has required them to nominate a body of aldermen, one-third as numerous as themselves and holding office twice as long. This was intended to add to the council men of high position who would not condescend to a popular election, but in practice the councillors commonly choose new aldermen—this election is held just after the council elections—by promoting senior members of their own body to fill the vacancies. Lastly, there is the mayor, elected annually by the council to preside over its deliberations. In those deliberations his office forbids him to take a partisan share, but he represents the town on all official occasions, entertains at the public—and his own—expense, and is automatically made a justice of the peace during his tenure of office. The actual work of the borough council we will consider separately.

Turning now to the government of the countryside, we find that the main authority is the county council, of which there are 62 for England and Wales, including 10 formed for divisions of counties, such as the three ridings of Yorkshire. This body is composed of a chairman, aldermen, and councillors, but although the franchise in the county (and its districts) is the same as in the boroughs, a county council differs from a borough council in three respects. All the councillors are elected at a single triennial election, so there is one to each district, who is much more of a local spokesman than is the representative of a ward in a town. Secondly, the county aldermen, thanks to lingering aristocratic traditions, are often chosen from outside the council. And thirdly, the chairman is less of a figurehead and often the moving spirit of the council's activities, a difference which may be partly explained by the fact that many ceremonial duties are discharged by the Lord Lieutenant, an official nominated by the crown as its titular representative in each county since Tudor days, when he commanded the militia. An important difference of another kind is that, whereas the police of a county borough are controlled by the watch committee, a committee of the council but one whose decisions the full council is not empowered to revoke, a county police force is ruled by a Standing Joint Committee. In this the justices of the peace have as many representatives as the county council, though the only other important administrative power they still retain is the granting of licences to publicans at brewster sessions.

A county council, indeed, labours under certain disadvantages. Distance makes frequent meetings inconvenient; the sparse population of the countryside and its poverty (together with some legal disabilities) deter the county councillors from launching out upon expensive projects; and country dwellers are naturally conservative. Moreover, although the main business of district councils is sanitation in the widest sense, from drainage to housing, rural as well as urban district councils inevitably discharge some functions which a county council might like to have under its own direct management, and even the R.D.C. is sometimes a very active subordinate. It is strong inasmuch as its members—usually one to each parish—represent collectively a small area, with the needs of which they are thoroughly conversant, the dominant element consisting usually of farmers. Financially, on the other hand, the R.D.C. is weak, since it is allowed to retain only a small part of the rates for its own use and is not encouraged to recoup itself by schemes of municipal trading: but since 1929 the position has been improved by relieving the R.D.C. (though not the U.D.C.) of any financial liability for the upkeep of the roads. This enables it to spend more on other objects, such as a local water supply, if it chooses.

Under the R.D.C. there is still the parochial organization, consisting of a half-yearly parish meeting and, wherever the population exceeds 300, a triennially elected parish council. Street lighting, the upkeep of footpaths, and the provision of a children's playing-field are three of the duties which a parish council commonly undertakes. There are many other things which it can easily get permission to do, but a rural parish, by the time it has paid its county and district rates, is usually not eager to seek opportunities for further communal expenditure. Perhaps the most important function of the meeting or council of a parish is to complain when the major councils prove neglectful.

3. HOW LOCAL COUNCILS DO THEIR WORK

The possible activities of a major local council are very numerous. Apart from the acts of 1835, 1888, and 1894, on which the system is based, parliament continued for many years to assign new duties to local government authorities, partly at least because laissez-faire traditions made it reluctant to involve the central government too closely in directing the economic and social life of the community. More recently, indeed, the trend has been in the opposite direction: the relief of the poor, for example, has passed almost entirely out of local hands. There is also a tendency to concentrate authority in the upper tier of the two-tier organization which prevails in the counties, so that the councils of municipal boroughs and urban and rural districts feel that the important work is withheld from them. But for county and county borough councils at least, many general powers remain. There are in addition some adoptive acts and many permissive clauses which entitle local authorities to undertake extra functions, chiefly in the field of amenities, if they choose. Moreover, almost every major authority has certain powers of its own, obtained by means of a local act or acts, which it has induced parliament to pass for its sole benefit. Accordingly, these activities will be reserved for a separate chapter, while we examine first certain common features in the way in which they are carried on.

Firstly, then, it is important to observe that all local authorities are strictly subordinate authorities. Everything they do must be brought within the four corners of some act of parliament, or it is illegal, and the high court, if appealed to, as it is sure to be sooner or later, will formally declare the action to be *ultra vires*. Conversely, if any act requires them to do something, and they omit to do it, the high court will order its performance by a writ of Mandamus. Furthermore, one of the largest government departments, the ministry of housing and local government, is constantly engaged in the task of supervising local authorities, advising, exhorting, inspecting, and—most vital of all—controlling and auditing their finances. Finally, in the important matter of making by-laws two sanctions are applied, for every local regulation of this kind must be both based upon a statute and authorized by the appropriate ministry.

The fact that they are subordinate deprives the local councils of the glamour which attaches to Westminster and partly explains a second feature—the comparative insignificance of party. In most large towns there is, indeed, a strong opposition between a Conservative side, which wishes to keep down local expenditure in the interests of the wealthier ratepayers, and a Labour or Socialist side, the policy of which is to use the rates to benefit the masses. Consequently, local elections are fought between the two political parties as a kind of rehearsal of a general election, and strong feelings may be aroused. Nevertheless, 50 per cent is a good poll in a local election; many councils (especially the smaller ones) have a number of non-party members; and in any case the voting does not invariably follow party lines. The office of mayor, for example, or a seat on the aldermanic bench may often go by rotation of some kind to a member of a party which happens to be in the minority.

The weakness of party, in turn, is closely connected with the prevalent system of government by committee. In a borough the council itself meets usually once a month, a county council only once a quarter (which is the legal minimum), and these meetings are formal and public. But they are largely devoted to the reception of reports from committees, which have been printed and circulated to members, and are now to be approved. Any member may then question the past actions or future intentions of a particular committee; its chairman will defend its conduct; and the vote of the whole council is legally decisive. It is the practice, however, except in very contentious matters, to accept what the committee does: hence the paramount importance of the committees, which in a big city like Birmingham or Manchester may total 30 or 40. Each member of the council will be assigned by vote to one or two of these, parties being represented on committees in rough proportion to their strength in the council as a whole. Where party feeling runs high, each chairman will represent the dominant party: but he is often elected by his committee merely because he is particularly keen and suited to the purpose. The committees meet more frequently and privately than the council, and it is there that the business is mainly transacted, under the guidance (and not merely the presidency) of the chairman, often with the help of persons with special knowledge co-opted from outside the council, and always with the expert assistance of an official.

This brings us to the last point. Councillors, after all, are unpaid amateurs, serving their constituents in what is often their scanty leisure: only the mayor or the chairman of the council may receive any allowance except for out-of-pocket expenses. In the nature of things, the average member is not a person of unusually wide experience or transcendent ability. Accordingly, a wise committee often defers to the chairman, and a wise chairman to the expert. The highest official of a council is its clerk, who is primarily a legal expert versed in the complicated legislation that governs the council's activities; but under his general authority there are a number of other officials. The minimum provision for a district council is a treasurer, medical officer of health and sanitary inspector (who may be the same person), and—except for a rural district with no road responsibilities delegated to it—a surveyor. But a major council must have other heads of departments, such as the chief constable and the education officer, and it may have as many as the number of its principal committees. Such men know their work, they know their subordinate staff, and they have a professional interest in producing the best possible results. Apart from broad questions of policy, therefore, which do not often arise, these officials, who are not much in the eye of the general public, are really the chief factor in ensuring good local government. Thus the American professor A. L. Lowell, after studying a number of English cities, was led to conclude that

> the excellence of municipal government was very roughly proportional to the influence of the permanent officials. That influence, be it observed, is by no means confined to matters where purely expert knowledge is required. By far the greater part of their work is administrative, and it is not too much to say that the administration of a typical English borough is conducted by the officials. . . . It is not the business of the committees of a borough council to work the departments, but to see that they are properly worked.[1]

What is here written of boroughs is no less true of counties, where greater distances may leave the official in even more unfettered control of his department.

[1] A. L. Lowell: *Government of England*, II, p. 179.

X

LOCAL GOVERNMENT SERVICES

1. A MATTER OF FINANCE

THE fundamental power of a local authority has always been the power to levy a local tax, paid by every householder, either directly or as an addition to his rent, the amount of which is proportionate to the value of his house. The valuation is in theory equal to the estimated annual rent, less cost of repairs, but it has tended to fall much below, partly at least because boroughs, urban districts, and rural districts—the authorities which collect the rates —also assessed rateable values throughout their area: the lower the total value, the smaller the proportion of county council expenditure which the area had to defray. Nowadays, however, the valuation is made by the inland revenue authorities. Suppose a house is valued at £40 *per annum*: if the local tax—the rates, as they are called—is declared one year to be '18 shillings in the £', then the householder in question will have to contribute £36. In the days when poor relief was the chief object on which rates had to be spent there was a great outcry among the well-to-do if rates were high; and within living memory there were many local authorities that tried to keep their total expenditure, including such items as lighting and cleaning the streets, as low as possible. But a gradual change of attitude has come about, from which have sprung many, perhaps most, of the public amenities that we all enjoy. These amenities in the opinion of most people are very much worth while: but it is important to remember that the new municipal park or the extension to the local library probably means that every householder has a little bit less of his income free to spend on himself and his family as he pleases. Thus in 1875 the rates amounted to £19,000,000 (less than £1 a head); in 1938 they stood at £191,000,000 (more than £4 10s. a head); and they now exceed £500,000,000 (more than £10 a head). Allowing for the fall in the value of money, in less than three generations the burden of the rates has certainly doubled.

There is, however, one important section of local government activities which may cost the ratepayer nothing. We allude to municipal trading enterprises—'municipal' because in a county area distance acts as a deterrent, not to mention the rigorous rule by which all expenditure above £100 requires to be estimated for by the finance committee. These enterprises usually began with the establishment, or the taking over from private hands, of the waterworks, water being supplied to every house for a fixed charge known as the water rate. Then they became extended, soon after the middle of the nineteenth century, to the supplying of light (first gas, then electricity), on the one hand, and of local transport (trams, later buses), on the other. In all these cases there were two strong arguments in favour of municipal ownership. Free competition among private firms was scarcely possible, since we could not have four water-mains or even four rival sets of buses running along the same street; and it was eminently in the public interest that the supply should be good and cheap. Thus the possibility of moving a part of the population from a slum area in the centre of the town to the outskirts might depend upon the provision of cheap transport, running on a margin of profit which a private firm would not consider adequate.

The position before the second world war was that these enterprises taken as a whole had a net loss of about £1,000,000 a year. Since then local authorities have been deprived of the gas and electricity undertakings, which (together with the control of markets) were their most profitable ventures. There have been considerable new developments in the fields of entertainment, provision for outdoor recreations, and catering facilities—British Restaurants were a wartime innovation—but it must be conceded that in most areas the advantages to the ratepayer are not mainly financial.

We may pass on to consider other means besides hypothetical commercial profits, by which the rates are supplemented. One of these, in a sense, is the flotation of loans. Every big new enterprise—a rehousing scheme, for instance—is financed by borrowing money from the general public, and the fact that no such stock can be issued without the express sanction of the government department concerned is the most important of the ways in which the ministry of housing and local government in particular keeps the whip hand over all local authorities. At the present moment local indebtedness would take the whole proceeds of the rates for nine years to repay; but as local bonds—unlike the national debt—require to be paid off in a short term of years, the system may be said to provide a large sum of ready cash rather than any long-term relief to the ratepayer.

Local authorities also receive government grants, the total of which nowadays exceeds what they raise from rates. When given as grants in aid of particular services, they act as an automatic check upon efficiency, which in the case of the police has operated for more than a century. In 1835 every borough, and in 1856 every county, was required to maintain a professional police force in place of the old amateur parish constables. But, apart from the metropolitan police, each of these forces was independent of the home office, whose function, it will be remembered, is nevertheless to maintain law and order throughout the country. The solution to the problem was found in an offer by the government to meet from national resources one-quarter of the cost of clothing and wages for every local force which reached a satisfactory standard of efficiency. By 1919 this had risen to one-half the cost of all approved police expenditure, subject to the same proviso. Since no watch committee and no county joint committee dare confront the ratepayers with an unnecessary loss, the word of Her Majesty's inspectors of constabulary, who can give or withhold the certificate of efficiency, is law throughout the police forces of the country. Similar percentage grants-in-aid have contributed to the progress of other local services, including those concerned with public health, housing, and education.

In 1958, however, the greater part of the government payments to local authorities was transferred to a new general grant, a lump sum fixed for two or three years in advance, which each authority could allocate as it pleased, subject only to the maintenance of 'reasonable standards'. This was designed both to give greater freedom and to discourage the extravagance which was said to be one of the results of the percentage grant system. We may notice, however, that the accounts of all local authorities have long been subject to a strict annual examination by the district auditors of the ministry, who have powers of surcharge.

As with a smaller block grant instituted thirty years earlier, an elaborate formula was devised, so that the proportion of the new general grant given to each authority should vary in accordance with such factors as population, age distribution (the under-15s and the over-65s are the biggest consumers of local services) and total rateable value. At the same time the rating of industrial property, which had been reduced to 25 per cent of the normal level in 1929, was raised to 50 per cent, so that local authorities should have rather more money apart from grants.

2. EDUCATION

Of the many services which the state operates through local authorities, none is more important or attracts more public attention than education. It is also by far the biggest rate-consuming service. In Hertfordshire, a home county with a large child population and a progressive attitude to education, the education budget for 1961–2 totalled £14,725,000, which was twelve times the cost of any other local service and nearly twice the amount of the general grant paid to the county council for all services. We find, accordingly, that administration must be through a statutorily prescribed committee of the council, which becomes the Local Education Authority or L.E.A. for a county or county borough. A county is divided into districts, within which many powers are delegated to a Divisional Executive nominated by the local district councils, while municipal boroughs and urban districts with populations of more than 6,000 are entitled to rank as Excepted Districts, which means that they have full control of their own schools but no concern with higher education. There is also a network of inspectors covering the whole country, who act as the eyes and ears and nose of the minister of education, to whom the act of 1944 gave 'control and direction of the national policy . . . in every area'.

If we omit private and preparatory schools at one end of the scale and the large public schools (expensive and influential but numerically insignificant) at the other, our schools are all—in a different sense of the word—public. Primary schools have been so since 1870, when the first education act instituted 'board schools' under locally elected school boards and at the same time gave increased subsidies to the existing voluntary schools built by the religious denominations, such as the Anglican 'national schools', if they conceded admission without religious obligation. Secondary schools under public control date only from the act of 1902. This law enabled new 'county schools' to be founded and existing grammar school foundations to be taken over step by step, as the 'free places' for which the local authority paid came gradually to be their main financial resource. In 1918 a third act gave some stimulus to the growth of free secondary education and made a little public money available to provide a further ladder to the university, but the biggest development between the wars was the introduction of the 'senior school' to provide separately for children of 11–14.

Since 1944 the educational ladder has become much wider; the upper rungs now form, indeed, a separate ladder such as earlier generations never knew. To begin at the bottom end, nursery schools are still lamentably few, especially in relation to the increased proportion of mothers with employment outside the home; but the commencement of primary school life at the fifth birthday nevertheless gives English children an earlier start than those of most other nations. After six years distributed between the infant and the junior stage, all children are now provided with a four-year secondary course, reaching to a minimum leaving age of 15, which may be raised to 16 without further legislation. There are three types of course—that given in the secondary modern school, which is not primarily academic and need not take account of outside examination requirements; that given in the not very numerous secondary technical schools; and in secondary grammar schools, with an academic bias and outside examinations. All grammar school education, except that provided in a very few schools that receive a direct grant from the ministry and are not subject to the local authority, is now entirely free of charge. But unfortunately there is still rather less of it than the country needs and very much less than parents ambitious for their children think the country ought to provide. Much criticism has therefore been directed against the 'eleven-plus' examination at the end of the junior school course, since this largely settles which type of school a child enters, and transfers at any later stage are difficult to arrange.

The London County Council and a number of other large urban authorities have sought to solve this and other social problems by building 'comprehensive schools' to comprehend all three types of secondary education in one gigantic organization, which has various advantages. Transfers within the comprehensive school should be easy to arrange at any stage. The thorough intermixing of social groups on the pattern of the American high school may be a sound democratic practice. The splendid equipment which is characteristic of these new institutions must act as a stimulus to the less gifted pupil and help to create a sense of corporate loyalty. The largeness of the unit, which needs to be somewhere near 2,000 pupils, may in some respects make administration easier. But it will take time and much patient leadership to establish the true ethos of a form of schooling which is almost completely new to the English scene.

The act of 1944 aimed at providing compulsory further education to the age of 18, which would bridge the gap or gulf between life at school and life at work by requiring one day a week to be spent at a 'county college': but sixteen years later these colleges were still waiting to be built. Vocational courses on a voluntary basis are provided by evening institutes, and local authorities also subsidize nonvocational classes, such as those of the workers' educational association and the university extension movement. These, however, make only a limited appeal to those who have left school at 15, while day-release schemes of any kind are still available to no more than a small minority of young people in employment.

The more academic type of school-leaver, who has profited by a sixth-form course in a grammar school, is much better provided for. Broadly speaking, scholarships (including state scholarships) and grants made by local authorities now enable any boy or girl who manages to secure a place at a university or comparable institution to take advantage of their chance. Since the number of university places has doubled in 15 years and is still being increased, chiefly through government funds administered by the independent University Grants Committee, the guess might be hazarded that the top intellectual stratum of the community is now given its due. There are, however, some possible exceptions—children of very poor parents who must make a contribution to the family income before the age of about 21, and those in some professional families which just fail to qualify in the means test for grants. Moreover, even the opening of three new English universities in the early 1960s will not solve the problem of the stratum next to the top, for which other countries such as America and Russia provide university places on a generous scale, in the expectation of high social and technological advantage to the community.

The work of local government in education does not end at the school gates. Museums and art galleries, such as every large town now maintains, do much and might do more to widen the outlook of the enquiring child. There has also been a big improvement in library services, particularly perhaps in rural areas: until 1919 the counties had no libraries at all, and the municipal ones were restricted to the produce of a penny rate. Finally, there are the youth services, for which grants-in-aid under the supervision of the board of education first became available in 1921. The importance which the 14–18 age group was seen to have for the nation during the second world war led, however, to a much more serious attempt to train youth leaders and to finance youth clubs, provided mainly by outside bodies such as the churches, so as to help them to fulfil some of the functions of informal further education. The delay in starting county colleges has added to the importance of clubs which shape the use of leisure.

3. HOUSING

Modern local government has always had to do with environmental services, which affect the conditions of living for every local citizen: the narrowly restricted municipal corporations act of 1835 at least gave powers for lighting and safeguarding the streets. Forty years later Disraeli's legislation, when it confirmed the town councils in the exercise of wide sanitary powers, which the more enterprising ones had already obtained by private bills—the control of drainage, water supply, measures against epidemics, etc., accepted without challenge ever since—also introduced the principle of local control over local building activities. In 1909 town planning powers were at last added, though only for undeveloped areas.

But results were meagre. Local authorities found that slum clearance involved not only trouble with landlords over the loss of easy profits but a burden on the rates, for compensation and cost of rehousing, which was not in those days readily acceptable to public opinion. Progress came chiefly through the adoption of by-laws setting minimum local standards of space, light, ventilation, and sanitation for all new construction. These were strengthened in 1890 by the Housing of the Working Classes Act—a significant name—and the by-law houses of the 'nineties, built in long monotonous rows with narrow gardenless frontages, were for the most part still habitable forty years later. The only instance of a fully planned urban community was Letchworth, and there the pioneer work of Ebenezer Howard was impeded by difficulties in the establishment of local industries, so that this first garden city, founded in 1903, came perilously near to the status of a mere dormitory town, with predominantly middle-class householders commuting daily to London.

It was in 1919 that housing first became a burning political issue: there had been no building during the war; costs had risen enormously; and so had people's expectations. Accordingly, subsidies were now provided for the construction, either by private enterprise or directly by local authorities, of working-class houses to a minimum specification, which provided for a bathroom and for a maximum density of 12 to the acre (eight in agricultural areas). The quantity built was impressive—about 4,000,000 in twenty years, of which local authorities built more than a quarter. The result in terms of a new standard of accommodation enjoyed by a large proportion of workers' families was also impressive. But even the provision in 1930 of special subsidies to help in slum clearance was far from finally solving the problem of how best to assist the type of family which had settled down in insanitary or overcrowded conditions or which contained an unusually large number of dependent children. These were the two categories for which the law offered preferential treatment in moving to a new house on a housing estate, but the move would normally involve both higher rent and additional fares to and from work. Planning also languished: in 1939, 95 per cent of the surface of England and Wales was still as providence and private enterprise had left it.

The second world war gave a great impulse to change. One reaction to the Blitz was a strongly emotional demand for some large-scale beneficial reconstruction of the devastated areas which would be the reward of victory. The war also brought about a social levelling, which both helped to produce a big comparative rise in the wages of slum-dwellers and also stimulated their aspirations towards higher social standards. Furthermore, the fact that rights of private property had not been allowed to stand in the way of the national war effort helped to produce a climate of opinion in which town and country planning at last became politically acceptable. Under an act of 1947 local authorities were enabled to plan the future use of land in advance, instead of waiting as in the past to allow or disallow some actual proposal. They could now develop any site themselves; no development could be made without their permission.

In 1951 a new ministry of housing and local government was formed, which took over everything except health from the ministry of health and absorbed a small ministry of town and country planning, which had been brought into existence before the end of the war. All development plans made by local authorities, as well as clearance orders and orders for compulsory purchase, require confirmation from this ministry, which employs a body of inspectors comparable to the factory inspectors. In each of the 11 standard regions, into which the treasury at the end of the war divided the country for purposes of departmental administration:

> the principal regional officer, assisted by architectural, engineering, planning, research and estate officers, has executive, supervisory, inspecting and advisory functions in connection with local authority housing programmes and their financing.[1]

There is thus a danger in this as in some other aspects of local government that central control may swamp local initiative.

As for results, the general housing subsidy which obtained for ten years after the war secured the completion of about 2,200,000 houses and flats, of which about two-thirds were built for local authorities. Subsidies for slum clearance still continue, as does financial aid for schemes to disperse population from congested areas in big cities into new satellite towns and others that may be suitable to receive an 'overspill' from elsewhere. Many difficulties

[1] L. P. Green: *Provincial Metropolis*, 1959, p. 150.

remain. Quite apart from vexed questions of aesthetic standards, there is the growing practical problem of how to make the best overall use of space on a crowded industrialized island. Space-consuming suburban housing estates continue to proliferate; flats in central areas provide a remedy for transport problems which English people, especially those with young families, accept with reluctance; and the propriety of applying a means test for the occupancy of rate-subsidized dwellings is a subject of continuing controversy in some districts. But the substantial achievements of the first thirty years of a national housing policy are registered in the late Aneurin Bevan's comment in 1950: 'The causes of the housing problem in Great Britain today are the higher social standards of the people.'

XI

THE GOVERNMENT OF LONDON

1. ELECTIVE AUTHORITIES

THERE are many reasons why the local government of London merits separate treatment. The capital of a kingdom and the historic centre of a great Commonwealth has a glamour all its own. A conglomeration of more than 8,000,000 souls (the present population of Greater London) offers peculiar problems to the civic legislator. The ancient City, embedded in the heart of this modern urban area, preserves forms and ceremonies from our remotest history. Above all, there is the awkward fact that the government of London even to-day is legally different from the types of provincial self-government which we have been studying. Some readers of this book no doubt live in London: but whether one happens to live there or not, the metropolis must interest and concern us all.

In the early nineteenth century the only London authority was that of the City Fathers: outside the square mile of the City about 300 small local bodies looked after the various needs of different parts of the ever-growing suburban area—each parish had a Vestry, and statutory authorities established under private acts of parliament looked after the lighting, cleaning, or paving of the streets. The result was chaos and corruption, which were first checked when the metropolitan police was established in

1829 and the reformed poor law unions in 1834. Then in 1855 a metropolitan board of works was instituted, which started the existing main drainage system along the Embankment and one of the first efficient municipal fire brigades, but never stood high in public reputation—perhaps because its members were elected, not by a popular vote, but indirectly through the old vestries and similar bodies. There matters rested for another generation, until the county councils act in 1888 set up a special form of county council for a narrowly defined county of London.

Although the L.C.C. was designed to function as the main local authority for the metropolitan area, the ancient City was allowed to remain for most purposes quite separate. Moreover, the area over which the L.C.C. had jurisdiction was not permitted to grow with the continued rapid growth of London. The new county inherited its boundaries from the old metropolitan board of works, roughly commensurate with the built-up area of the 1880s. But other parts of the four neighbouring home counties, into which London spread subsequently, remained under the rule of their respective county—and three county borough—councils, together with 38 borough councils and other subordinate authorities. The new county contained to begin with none of the county subdivisions set up in 1894, but five years later Lord Salisbury's third ministry, which is said to have found too small an element of conservatism in L.C.C. policies, subdivided it into 28 new metropolitan boroughs (including Westminster, later elevated to city status) with a special constitution of their own. Thus London came to contain three forms of council peculiar to itself as well as specimens of all the forms found elsewhere; yet it had no council to represent the whole of the modern metropolitan area—an anomaly for which remedies were being actively sought and discussed from 1921 onwards.

The L.C.C. has a large number of councillors, namely three for each of its 42 electoral divisions, which are the same as the parliamentary constituencies for London, but it has only one-sixth as many aldermen. It may also be organically distinguished from great county boroughs such as Manchester or Birmingham by the fact that it is headed by a chairman and holds triennial general elections. The council meets fortnightly and in public, but as in other councils the work is done mainly in committees, of which there are 14, meeting fortnightly and—except for the education committee—in private. The L.C.C. has always been organized on party lines, each committee having a chairman and vice-chairman representing the majority party, who work together under a leader of the council. The scope of the duties to be discharged distinguishes the L.C.C. from other county councils in two ways: by their size, since provision has to be made for a tightly packed population of about 3,200,000 at a cost (including debt charges) of about £80,000,000 a year; and to some extent also by their nature. Responsibility for education and welfare services, for example, is not shared with any other local authority. As a metropolitan authority the L.C.C. has always taken its educational duties very seriously: the new comprehensive schools already mentioned illustrate this, as does the support long given to London university and every form of higher education. As an authority responsible for vast areas of slums and quasi-slums, it has attacked housing problems by drastic methods, such as the purchase of land far outside the county for the development of housing estates, like that at Becontree in Essex, or the buying-up of property within the county on the gigantic scale that will enable two-thirds of the entire borough of Stepney to be redeveloped in one generation. Access to open spaces for recreation presents another acute difficulty to Londoners, which their council has mitigated by making grants of something like £2,000,000 to enable neighbouring authorities to secure land for a green belt not too far distant from the congested central region.

The metropolitan borough councils consist of mayor, aldermen, and councillors, as in other boroughs, but the proportion of aldermen and the incidence of elections is as in the L.C.C. All 28 are linked together by a standing joint committee. The duties are mainly those of other non-county borough councils, but drainage, housing, and the provision of parks and open spaces—all matters of special difficulty in inner London—are dealt with partly by the L.C.C.

The corporation of the City of London is a unique local authority and one of the most venerable of all existing British institutions. The municipal corporations act of 1835 was not allowed to touch the privileges of the city, where the mediaeval guilds or livery companies have continued into the twentieth century as a combination of dining club and charity, there being in many cases considerable revenues, which go to maintain schools and occasionally the technical standards of the trade with which they were once associated. Their members are the liverymen, about 10,000 in all, who as freemen of the city help to elect its principal dignitaries, the lord mayor and sheriffs and the finance officer or chamberlain. Aldermen and councillors, on the other hand, are elected for each ward by residents and—a far more numerous body—non-resident occupants of premises worth not less than £10 a year.

The 25 aldermen, elected for life, form a kind of upper house, which joins with the 159 common councilmen,[1] who are elected annually, to constitute the court of common council: this is the governing body of the city. In addition to the powers which it shares with the metropolitan borough councils, the city administers its own police force and police courts, with a recorder and two other judges (who also sit at the Old Bailey); controls all markets within seven miles of its boundaries; and profits from estates to an annual value of £660,000.

2. OTHER METROPOLITAN INSTITUTIONS

The size and complexity of London's problems and its position as both a political and commercial capital of long standing have caused it to be prolific in organizations which control local services without being directly responsible to any local electorate.

The oldest of these is the metropolitan police, and it is at first sight surprising that the force established by Peel in 1829, having served in other respects as a model both for the borough police and the county police, stands by itself in its direct subordination to the home secretary. He appoints the commissioner, who, with the help of a deputy and four assistant commissioners, commands an organization which musters about one-fourth of all the police in England and Wales. The district they patrol includes all parishes within 12 miles of Charing Cross and small areas beyond: it is about six times as large as the county of London and two and a half times as populous. Half the

[1] Reduction to this total will be completed in December 1965.

cost is paid by local authorities, which nevertheless have no say in the administration. The anomaly is commonly defended on the score of the special need for police efficiency in a capital city. The other argument used in Peel's day was the chaotic condition of local government as administered by vestries: the vestries have gone long since, but the metropolitan police district still lacks any single elective authority which could claim to administer the police.

The port of London authority, set up by Lloyd George in 1908, controls the port installations, docks, and tidal waters of the Thames from Teddington to the sea. A clear majority of its members, who serve for three years at a time, are chosen by payers of dues, wharfingers, and owners of river craft, a system which takes little account of general public interests but is calculated to secure efficiency in the working of the port. Two other authorities concerned with the river are the Thames Conservancy, which regulates the upper reaches—once numbered among the duties of the lord mayor—and the Metropolitan Water Board, which draws from the Thames about two-thirds of the supply for an area almost as large as the police district. Both of these are indirectly democratic in constitution, since a majority of members represent the different local councils of their area. In 1933, however, when a London Passenger Transport Board was instituted 'to secure the provision of an adequate and properly co-ordinated system of transport', the labours of Sisyphus were to be performed by the nominees of five appointing trustees, among whom only the chairman of the L.C.C. represented the local councils. At the present day those thankless labours are continued by the London Transport Board, attempting to co-ordinate all the underground and surface services by

Other Metropolitan Institutions

which the population is poured into and out of central London from distances up to a 25-mile radius. Intimately as their work affects the life of every Londoner, both whole- and part-time members are nominated by the minister of transport.

These London areas, so various in size and definition, are all linked together by the influence of transport developments upon their affairs. In the nineteenth century the growth of new forms of transport was what enabled the night-time population of the City to shrink: nowadays it is less than one per cent of those who make their living in the square mile by day. So also in the twentieth century relations between the L.C.C. and outer London authorities are largely governed by the fact that Londoners prefer the inconvenience of long daily journeys to the feeling of complete divorce from even a suburban countryside.

Thus the London area provides the biggest of several problems of unsatisfactory conurbations in Britain, and in London as elsewhere drastic efforts are being made to ease the situation by removing families into remoter local government areas. Since 1946 this has been done under the New Towns Act, which speaks for itself, and since 1952 by the Town Development Act, which enables existing small towns to form a nucleus for the resettlement of surplus population from a big city. London has sponsored the creation of six new towns. These will eventually have the normal form of local self-government: but the difficult early stages are entrusted to Development Corporations, whose members are appointed by the ministry of housing and local government. They normally include leading figures in the local government of the London area from which population is to be induced to move, and it is their job to acquire the land and initiate the necessary services. Transplantation is no easy business. But there is something inspiring in the thought of so ancient a community striking new roots elsewhere at the same time as the clearance of congested central areas breathes new life into the older stock.

XII

THE PUBLIC WORK OF WOMEN

1. HISTORICAL

AT the last census the women of the United Kingdom outnumbered the men in every adult age-group. This preponderance of women, which occurs in most countries, provides an additional justification—if any is needed—for an attempt to give here a summary account of the vast change in their position as citizens, which has been brought about in the last hundred years.

A century ago the legal rights of women were practically non-existent. In private life the married woman at least had next to no control over her own property or her own children: *a fortiori* there was no room for women in the control of public affairs. Their eligibility to the boards of guardians constituted in 1834 was the only apparent exception—apparent because no female guardian was in fact elected until 1875. Florence Nightingale's career showed clearly enough what a woman could contribute to public life, but her miracles of organization in the Crimea were so to speak explained away on the ground that nursing was naturally a female occupation. At all events, no serious attempt to change the situation was made until 1867, when the utilitarian philosopher, John Stuart Mill, who constituted himself the first important champion of women's rights, moved an amendment to Disraeli's parliamentary reform bill of that year, proposing to extend the franchise to women. The amendment received 80 votes, and thereafter the question of the parliamentary vote was never allowed to sleep: but for the next forty years the progress made was in two other directions. By a series of laws beginning in 1870 the position of married women in relation to their property was gradually transformed; and by the 'seventies the movement in favour of higher education for women, which began with Queen's college, London, in 1848, had reached an important stage by the foundation of colleges at Cambridge and Oxford. Economic and intellectual prepared the way for political independence. Already the doors of opportunity in local government were being allowed to swing open. The municipal franchise was conferred on women ratepayers in 1869, and the county franchise was theirs from the inauguration of the councils in 1888. What perhaps mattered more was the right to be elected. Women were admitted to the school boards in 1870, to district and parish councils in 1894, and finally to borough and county councils in 1907.

By the last of these dates, however, a new interest was being roused in the question of the parliamentary franchise through the foundation of Emmeline Pankhurst's social and political union in 1903 and the determined leadership which she gave it. This was the movement which gained enormous notoriety by a campaign of violence, intended to attract attention (in which it certainly succeeded) and to force the hand of the Asquith government (in which it was apparently less successful). What its ultimate results would have been we cannot tell. In 1914 the war intervened, the energies of militant suffragettes and their more law-abiding sisters were diverted to war work, and the gift of the franchise in 1918 was supposed to be the reward of the latter: though fear of the revival of militancy may well have played a part in the government's decision.

At all events, the Representation of the People Act gave the vote to women ratepayers and wives of ratepayers if above the age of thirty, and another statute of the same year entitled them also to sit as members of the house of commons. In 1919 the Sex Disqualification (Removal) Act laid down the general principle that women, whether married or unmarried, were to be deemed fit to exercise any public function: this covered, for example, the right to take part in legal proceedings as magistrates, advocates, and members of a jury. Finally, the Equal Franchise Act in 1928 abolished the age-limit and other restrictions, so that women received the vote on exactly the same terms as men.

Nevertheless, three types of disqualification still remain. One of these is based on religious and moral principles of uncertain validity: the former prevent the established church from admitting women to its priesthood, the latter have restricted their role in the armed forces to non-combatant duties. The second is the tendency, common to the state and most types of private employer, to give lower rates of pay to women even when they are doing exactly the same work as men. Since the second world war both the government and the trades union congress have pledged their support for the principle of equal pay for equal work: but women in industry still earn on an average about two-thirds of a man's hourly wage, and teaching is perhaps the first of the bigger professions to achieve full equality between the sexes. Lastly, there is a curious legal anomaly. Although, by a practice dating back to the Tudor reigns, the throne may be inherited by, as well as through, a woman, yet a peeress in her own right is incapable of sitting in the house of lords. Such peeresses are only two dozen in all, and the justice of their claim was formally acknowledged by the lords themselves in 1949; but rectification of the anomaly is apparently to be left until the long-postponed reform of the upper house eventually takes place.

2. SOME ACHIEVEMENTS

Although there are now more women voters than men, the result has not been a great change in the composition of the house of commons. The number of female M.P.s has never yet risen above 24—not quite 4 per cent of the whole—a fact which is partly attributable to the reluctance of party organizations, run on traditional lines, to give women constituencies where the party has much chance of winning: nearly twenty years after their emancipation rather more than half the women candidates in an election were said to have been fighting 'forlorn hopes'. In the house itself they have been more active than the average member, for their sex still gives them a certain prominence; women are included (as we have seen) among the first of the new life peers; and they have reached cabinet rank as ministers of labour and education. Nevertheless, it is reasonable to suppose that more than one generation must elapse, during which women are educated to think of themselves as voters, before female representation takes full effect. But in the meanwhile, we may point to some examples of social reforms which have undoubtedly been aided by the women's vote. In 1925 pensions were conceded to widows, with additional allowances for each dependent child; it is significant that the family allowances in 1945 were made payable to the mother; and a whole series of acts have been brought in to safeguard the position of children in matters to do with adoption, employment, illegitimacy, and delinquency.

In local government, of which they have had longer experience, women play a more prominent part. 'Her Worship the Mayor' has ceased to be the butt of popular witticisms; women are commonly to be found in the chair of the education, child welfare, and similar committees; and the L.C.C. has about one-third women members, though this is well above the national average. Admission to the magistracy has also borne fruit, for there are now about 2,000 women J.P.s out of a total of 23,000. In the courts, as on the local councils, women have a special work to do, since the type of woman who is appointed or elected has usually undertaken some voluntary philanthropic activity earlier on, which tends to give her a better insight than the successful business man or territorial magnate into the lives and troubles of the poor. It is now officially recommended that a juvenile court should, wherever possible, include a woman magistrate.

In the professions women have extended their sphere from teaching and medicine, where alone they were to be found in any numbers before the war, to practically everything. They figure in the list of recorders and of queen's counsel, have had charge of British embassies abroad, and are at the head of at least two departments in the home civil service. At a different level, nursing has always been women's work: one result of their enfranchisement is an improvement in its status. The health service in general is now thrown open to them, and they are commonly found acting as sanitary inspectors and health visitors. The women police are, as an institution, more prominent:

suffice it to say that their services in the protection of women and children are so obviously valuable that a total of about 2,500, one-fifth of whom are in the metropolitan police, appears inadequate.

In the war of 1939–45 British women made a larger proportionate contribution to the national effort than the women of any other country, the USSR only excepted. Nearly half a million performed non-combatant duties as members of the armed forces, and another million and a half provided additional labour to replace the men withdrawn from industrial life. One consequence has been a permanent rise in the proportion of the female population having outside employment to nearly one-third. It has been well said that women 'though still regarding the home as the centre of their well-being . . . no longer regard it as their boundary'.[1] This is a social change of the utmost importance to men and children as well as to the women themselves.

Nevertheless, it is not in paid service or even in official life that women have hitherto made their most valuable contribution to the state. Under pre-war conditions one-fifth of the women in the country occupied no salaried post at any time in their lives, and of the remainder a high proportion gave up their posts on marriage and might find themselves, sooner or later, with a good deal of leisure on their hands. Hence the number and magnitude of the voluntary activities for the public benefit which their efforts have sustained. We have only space to distinguish three types. First, work by women for women: the best example of this is perhaps the network of 8,000 women's institutes, established all over the country during the

[1] Conservative Women Reform Group's pamphlet, quoted by V. Douie: *Daughters of Britain* (1949), p. 158.

inter-war years, which have done much to deprive village life of drabness and torpor. There is also the national council of women, now a body with very wide social interests, but founded in 1895 for the protection of friendless girls. Secondly, there is the organization of charity, about which more will be said in the next chapter: here we need only notice that the W.V.S., set up in 1938 in anticipation of air bombing—the full name is Women's Voluntary Services for Civil Defence—has developed into a most valuable instrument of social aid in peacetime emergencies as well. Lastly, there is the special devotion which women have shown to the cause of internationalism: this first found expression in the league of nations union after the first world war and has been the backbone of every movement for world peace and disarmament since.

XIII

SOCIETIES WITHIN THE STATE

1. THE CHURCHES

EVERY citizen of the United Kingdom is necessarily concerned to some extent with the institutions so far described in this book: even if he never votes in parliamentary or local elections, the activities of central and local government directly affect him and the rules they make are legally binding upon him. But the state in the British view serves mainly as a framework within which the individual should be free to conduct his life as he pleases, partly on his own or as a member of a family, but partly also through the social groupings to which he chooses to belong. These groups are numerous and very varied—for most of us they include, for instance, the organization in which we earn our living—but we shall consider here only a very few types of society that, by virtue of their size or objects or both, have a marked influence upon the state. Indeed, some of the institutions of the state cannot be properly understood without taking such societies into account.

Pride of place must be given to the Christian churches, of which the membership was for about a thousand years conterminous with the state, except in so far as mediaeval kings up to Edward I chose to tolerate the presence in the country of a handful of Jews. At the reformation the protestant church of England 'as by law established' took the place of the church of Rome as a society of which every citizen was legally a member. The first permanent modification came in 1689. Since the toleration act of that year the four main factors leading to the present-day situation have been the growth of the protestant nonconformist or dissenting churches, especially after the start of the methodist movement in 1739; the survival of the church of Rome in England and its rapid increase in numbers when the industrial revolution brought the great influx of Irish; the immigration of persecuted Jews; and since the close of Victoria's reign, a marked and rapid rise in the proportion of the population that professes no religion at all.

The church of England with nearly 2,900,000 adult members registered on parochial church rolls in 1961, and about half that number of Sunday School children, is still an established church in England, but no longer in northern Ireland or Wales, while north of the border the presbyterian church of Scotland has been established continuously since 1690. Establishment gives additional dignity and brings about the adherence in a very passive way of the many persons who are baptized and confirmed in the church of England for reasons of tradition and family custom: 50 per cent of all marriages are still celebrated within its walls. It also gives the church a prescriptive right to make its voice heard, either from the episcopal bench in the house of lords or perhaps more effectively through the press and television, on any and every issue concerning public duty or private morals.

Its present-day organization is a tangle of compromises. The Queen, by virtue of the first statute passed in the reign of her great namesake, is 'Supreme Governor of this realm . . . as well in all spiritual or ecclesiastical things or causes as temporal'. In virtue of a still older arrangement, archbishops, bishops, and deans are elected by cathedral chapters under a *congé d'élire* from the crown accompanied by a letter naming the candidate to be chosen. In practice, this means that the higher offices in the church are filled in accordance with the wishes of church leaders, pre-eminently the archbishop of Canterbury, in so far as the prime minister does not advise the crown differently. As for control of the lower clergy, the incumbent or parish priest is presented with his living by a patron, who may still be a layman such as the village squire (though he must nowadays secure the acquiescence of the parochial church council, or failing that the bishop); moreover, the book of common prayer and the thirty-nine articles of religion provide the parson with a standard of observance which only a parliament of laymen is legally entitled to alter. But the clergy also have their ancient convocation, composed of separate houses of bishops and representatives of lower clergy in each of the two provinces of Canterbury and York, where matters of interest are debated; and since 1919 convocation has joined with a house of laity to form the church assembly, which prepares ecclesiastical measures for submission to parliament. There they will be considered by the ecclesiastical committee of lords and commons, and are either passed or rejected without possibility of amendment.

The finances of the church of England also represent a compromise between old and new. The cathedrals and the older parish churches derive part of the stipends of their clergy from ancient property rights, which are the prime reason for the great and seemingly unchristian disparity in clerical incomes. The position is to some extent ameliorated by the activities of the church commissioners, who dispose of a sum of about £14,000,000 a year derived from church estates and other assets. But the newer parishes resemble the congregations of unestablished churches in their more complete dependence upon the voluntary offerings of their members, as is also the case in the 280 Anglican dioceses overseas. These dioceses are not established in their own countries, whether inside or outside the Commonwealth, and have no constitutional dependence upon the mother see of Canterbury, though their spiritual unity finds clear expression in the decennial Lambeth conferences of the whole church.

The church of Scotland is governed by its annual general assembly, at which the sovereign is ceremonially represented by a lord high commissioner, while the moderator or president for the year ranks on Scottish soil as next after the lord chancellor. Like the church of England, it is the national church and endowed as such, but lay patronage of livings, which had been the cause of several secession movements, was finally abolished in 1874. The two outstanding features are the combination of ministers with lay elders in all the governing bodies of the church from the kirk session upwards, and the reunion of virtually all Scottish protestants which was achieved when the main seceding church came back in 1929.

The methodist, congregationalist, and baptist churches of England and Wales are directed and financed entirely by their own members: the strongest central organization is that of the methodists, while the congregationalists, as their name implies, believe in absolute local autonomy as most conducive to purity of worship. These and various smaller protestant bodies are linked together by the free church federal council, representing a regular membership rather more than half as large as the regularly worshipping membership of the church of England. The number of

Roman Catholics in England and Wales is estimated by the *Catholic Directory* on a different basis at more than 3,400,000. They are divided into four archbishoprics and 14 bishoprics, but the religious orders and societies which play a large part in their church life are not specifically British.

The churches were once the source of all education and all charity. Since the act of 1870 church schools have naturally come to play a smaller part, except in the case of Roman Catholics. Charitable work, too, is now performed by many other bodies, though few of them rival the salvation army and the quakers, for instance, as leaders in this field of activity. For while secular organizations may now command bigger resources, the churches are still the means by which a moral and altruistic point of view is most readily brought to bear on public questions—for the healing of international relations, for the expression of practical sympathy with oppressed peoples, work on marital and family problems, the care of unprotected childhood and old age, and the struggle against that poverty of the mind and spirit which has partly replaced the physical poverty our fathers knew.

2. TRADE UNIONS

Societies within the state often act upon it by organizing themselves as pressure groups, which seek to influence those in authority directly or by appealing to public opinion, perhaps through a lavish expenditure upon advertisement. The churches agitate for parliamentary action in support of faith and morals; trade associations work for the maintenance of a tariff or a monopoly; and professional bodies commonly try to obtain a charter which will exclude competition by unqualified outsiders. But none now plays so big a part as the trade union movement, which began in this country in the earliest phases of the industrial revolution as the almost blind reaction of oppressed workers against the overwhelming power of their employers.

When the trades union congress came into existence in 1868 to defend their interests on a national basis, the unions were just emerging from a long initial period of small strength, modest achievements, and little public repute. In 1871 trade unions were for the first time given a satisfactory legal status; in 1874 two of their leaders appeared as pioneer representatives in the house of commons; and in 1889 the London dock strike showed the possibility of successful action even by unskilled casual labour, given adequate leadership and propaganda. At that time the British trade union movement was ahead of the continent, to say nothing of America; in the new century other countries began to catch up with Britain, but solid gains were still obtained—a privileged legal status in 1906, protection for their political expenditure in 1913, and a vast increase in membership during the first world war. If the failure of the general strike and the prevalence of unemployment weakened their position during the inter-war period, the second world war more than restored their numbers, and the nationalization and other measures of the Labour government that followed gave to much of their long-term programme the force of law. Since the trade unions are the largest constituent element in the Labour party, whose leaders are expected to heed mandates emanating from the rank and file, they are almost a state within a state.

Their membership of more than 8,000,000 makes them a force to be reckoned with in every electoral campaign.

At the same time the economic pressure they can exert upon the individual employer, to say nothing of the individual employee who falls foul of them, is enormous. It is even possible for the state itself to be driven to capitulate to a key union, such as those controlling power supply or transport, when it seeks to gain its ends by using the strike weapon to inflict disproportionate hardship and loss upon the general public or upon industries not involved in the dispute. Nevertheless, the experience of the 1950s was that the impact of the unions on the state was ceasing to satisfy their members. It had been found that to nationalize an industry did not necessarily lead to any improvement as regards solvency, efficiency, or even harmonious internal relations. Strikes were seen to inflict much undeserved suffering upon the working class, to which strikers were naturally sensitive. Above all, there was a feeling that the officials of the huge unions of the less-skilled workers, which were now predominant, were hopelessly remote from the needs and ambitions of ordinary members, and that the latter were not always well represented even at the local level by branch committees and shop stewards who had private ends to serve.

But if we consider the trade unions in relation to their history, present weaknesses seem to be to some extent the result of past successes, which revolutionized the whole position of the worker in the community. The average worker no longer feels any burning sense of injustice: his thoughts dwell more readily upon the various opportunities now at his disposal for enjoying the fruits of his labours. This view is corroborated by the contrast between the present fortunes of two other types of society, which have grown up alongside the trade unions to serve the needs of the worker. Since the introduction of the national health service the voluntary friendly societies have lost about one-quarter of their members, who no longer see the same defenceless future ahead of them. In the same period consumers' co-operative societies, whose stores have never attracted the very poor (because they give no credit) but thrive upon mass prosperity, have increased their membership by about the same proportion, while the amount spent in the stores has more than doubled.

3. ORGANIZATIONS FOR SOCIAL SERVICE

The work of the churches has always included social service, but that was not the object for which they were founded. The working-class groups which we have just been describing, on the other hand, have had self-help as the prime mover rather than the deliberate desire to help others. For the beginning of social service in a rather narrower sense, the rendering of assistance by those not in need to those in need through specially planned societies, we might turn to the great eighteenth-century philanthropists, who organized hospitals and dispensaries for the sick, Sunday schools for the children of the poor, or relief for the inmates of prisons. But men such as Guy, Coram, Raikes, and Howard were very largely individualist in their approach to the problems of their day. Lord Shaftesbury's activities in the ragged school movement, which he joined in 1843, come closer to the notion of an effectively organized society. By 1867 there were 200 of these schools in London with an average attendance of 100 apiece, and both Dr. Barnardo's Homes and the National Children's Home and Orphanage were founded in that decade to serve the same pitiable need—that of the homeless waif, the flotsam and jetsam of the great city.

Nevertheless, the main Victorian landmark is the foundation in 1869 of the C.O.S., the 'society for the organization of charitable relief and the repression of mendicity'. The last phrase in the title is a reminder that the society also had the negative object of opposing all indiscriminate charity, as likely to do more harm than good: those were days when Smiles's *Self-help* stood close to the Bible in the bookshelves of the prudent. The positive principles were three—the belief that the family unit and not merely the needy individual required careful diagnostic study; the stern acceptance of the supposition that failures of character were the root cause of a mass of poverty which might properly be left to the harsh medicine of the poor law; and the determination, even within the restricted category of the deserving poor, to concentrate relief upon such cases as had a good chance of recovering complete independence. The help given was well intentioned and clearly systematic, though its sum total was almost insignificant in relation to the mass of misery that still went unrelieved. But one notable result was the pioneer work in housing management undertaken by Octavia Hill, who was a leading spirit in the C.O.S. Collecting the rents of two-room tenements in houses bought for the benefit of the poor, she was able to encourage thrift and assist a family to better its condition. Another result was the emergence of the idea that the upward urge, especially as regards cultural aspirations, would be stimulated if representatives of the more fortunate elements of society came to live for a time among the less fortunate: hence the university settlement movement, which began with the transplantation of Oxford men to Toynbee Hall in Whitechapel in 1884.

But a great gulf separates us from the Victorian social

order, in which the hardships of poverty were seen by those who were not poor as being for the most part a salutary chastisement and in any case a condition like the weather, for which the state could not be expected to take any responsibility. The wretchedly low standard of the national physique, as disclosed by recruitment for the South African war of 1899–1902, is said to have shaken the old complacency: at all events, it was about then that the cumulative process of change set in, by which the whole outlook on voluntary social service has been transformed. Instead of there being a huge mass of extreme poverty and suffering, from which a small portion is to be singled out for relief, the mass is altogether smaller and is held in check by the state services which have replaced the deterrent poor law. Voluntary social service thus operates in a much more manageable field, and even there it is open to the challenge: why should not this work, if it is necessary, be done by the state? The question is put all the more readily inasmuch as state services defrayed from the taxes diminish the resources that can readily be made available for private charity.

Health, educational opportunity, employment—these basic needs are now seen to demand provision by the state on a vast scale, for even the idea that finding work is primarily an individual responsibility died a lingering death during the great slump of the 1930s. But the wide ramifications of the service of youth and old age are still seen to require many forms of help with which the ponderous organization of central and local government cannot readily cope. Voluntary societies operate supplementary services, ranging from the care committees which for many years have made informal contacts with the homes of troubled schoolchildren in the metropolis to such W.V.S.

activities as bring hot meals to the pensioner who can no longer fend for himself. They are in a better position than the state to work discreetly and flexibly or experimentally: such considerations apply, for instance, to many of the activities of the inspectors of the NSPCC or to the kind of assistance rendered by the distressed gentlefolk's aid association. The youth club and the old people's home may be instanced as types of organization of growing importance to the community and backed extensively by public funds, which nevertheless require the help of voluntary workers if they are to succeed.

The fact that the state now plays a large part in all the social services has had the further important effect that there has ceased to be a clear line of demarcation between those who give and those who receive. In this respect the upheavals produced by bombing during the war years marked an important stage in social development in Britain, for the emergency services were often both needed and welcomed by comparatively well-to-do families. The fact that salaried workers figure more prominently in social work of all kinds may help efficiency: it certainly helps the sense of equality by contrast with the old conception of a Lady Bountiful. A village hall, built with a public grant made on the recommendation of a public official, may be physically the same as, but its social impact will be very different from, a hall endowed by the local squire in the old days. Part of the price to be paid for a healthier atmosphere is the complexity of the modern relationship between state and voluntary institutions, which is well illustrated by the activities of the National Council of Social Service. This came into existence in 1920 as a planning body, in which representatives of government departments and local authorities were to join with those of the voluntary organizations: about half the funds which it distributes come from private benevolence, the other half being made up of government grants for specific purposes. The outlook of a new era is shown in the fact that from the outset the proclaimed purpose of this influential body has been

> co-operation as the "rule" of social service. The old-fashioned conception of social work as an effort to help other people must give place to a new conception of social service as the common effort to achieve social well-being.[1]

[1] *Social Science Review*, Vol. I, No. 11.

XIV

THE COMMONWEALTH

1. IMPERIAL REVOLUTION

THE empire over which Queen Victoria had presided, the empire of the history books, reached its largest extent and the apogee of its power and influence at the close of the first world war. Although the self-governing dominions, no less than the Indian empire, had been involved without prior consultation by the British declaration of war, all had made important contributions to victory. That victory appeared to secure the empire against any further German menace by land or sea, and the total British service to the Allied cause entitled her to take what she wished from the defeated empires of Germany and the Ottoman Turks. Palestine, Mesopotamia, and Trans-Jordan, German East and South-West Africa with part of Togoland and the Cameroons, German New Guinea and Samoa all became mandates of Britain or British dominions—a form of control by the league of nations which placed them for the time being effectively within the empire. Moreover, Egypt had been declared a British protectorate in December 1914, soon after her suzerain Turkey had chosen the side of Britain's enemies, a fact which had even given rise to dreams of a third viceroyalty, that of the middle east, to be added some day to the Irish and the Indian. There had also been the forward-looking experiment of Lloyd

George's imperial war cabinet, when for two periods in 1917 and 1918 the five dominion prime ministers sat with the five United Kingdom members in a single directing body, though only the latter sat there with any formal responsibility to a parliament.

But the climax was likewise the turning-point. So far from there being any continuance of the imperial war cabinet, the dominions insisted upon separate representation at the peace conference—even though they signed the peace treaty collectively in the name of the empire—and more firmly and completely in the league of nations. By 1922 Egypt had ceased to be a protectorate, though it was still attached to Britain by a treaty of alliance which secured the control of the Suez canal. Nearer home, the Irish rebellion derived some of its unexpected strength from the sympathy expressed by an America whose power Britain was just beginning to realize, and was only terminated by the grant of dominion status to southern Ireland in the treaty signed in December 1921. If Britain could be successfully defied from across St. George's channel, at a greater distance also the forces of discontent might well find that under post-war conditions violence paid. Palestine, Malta, and Cyprus were smaller areas in which unrest made itself felt, but it was in India that the rapidly rising tide of nationalism presented British administration with its most intractable problems.

Self-government by stages had been promised in 1917, but within five months after the armistice political agitation and its repression culminated in the never-forgotten massacre of Amritsar, where the murder of some Europeans led to misconceived measures for dispersing an unlawful assembly, by which 359 Indians were shot dead. In December of the same year (1919) the government of

India act was belatedly passed, a first instalment towards fulfilling the promise made two years previously of

> the increasing association of Indians in every branch of the administration and the gradual development of self-governing institutions, with a view to the progressive realization of responsible Government in British India as an integral part of the British Empire.[1]

What this programme meant in practice was the setting up of an Indian legislature of two houses, which could pass laws and vote taxes but might always be overridden by the viceroy and his officials in the event of a deadlock. In the provinces a more genuine parliamentary system was evolved, known as diarchy, by which the work of administration was divided into two halves—'transferred subjects', which were under the charge of a native minister responsible to the legislative council, and 'reserved subjects' (such as the maintenance of law and order), on which the governor and his officials kept their hand. At the same time more Indians were recruited for the higher ranks of the civil service and for commissions in the army.

The sequel was an almost incessant agitation for complete home rule, *alias* dominion status, which led to the appointment of a series of commissions and conferences, and finally to the new Government of India Act of 1935. One main feature was full self-government in the provinces, where all ministers were to be made responsible to a provincial parliament and the governor was expected to use his power of veto very sparingly. The other main feature was a promising scheme for a federal system, with an all-India legislature, to which ministers would be re-

[1] Statement by the secretary of state, house of commons, 20 August 1917.

sponsible (except for some special viceroy's powers), linking the provinces with the native states. But in 1939 the federation was still in the making, because of India's religious divisions and the reluctance of her native princes.

As regards the dominions, however, a new concept of the meaning of empire was being developed in the 1920s, with its emphasis on equality. The veteran statesman and philosopher, A. J. Balfour, drew up a definition for the imperial conference of 1926, which five years later was embodied in the United Kingdom statute of Westminster. Great Britain and the dominions were declared to be 'autonomous communities within the British Empire, equal in status, in no way subordinate to one another', and the statute gave point to the declaration by expressly repudiating any limitation through laws of the United Kingdom of the absolute law-making powers of dominion governments. The treaty-making power had been formally granted earlier (1923) and there followed by slow degrees the establishment of separate diplomatic representation of dominions at key capitals, a fact which might demonstrate their sovereign status to the world.

But it was equality within unity—a unity clearly resting upon a common allegiance to the crown, but not upon that alone. Shortly before his death in 1930 Balfour made the following note:

> Whence comes the cohesion of the British Empire?
> 1. Patriotism. Loyalty. Custom.
> 2. Religion. Race. Pride in various manifestations. Habit. Language.
> *Mere* law is the weakest of all bonds.[1]

[1] Letter of Mrs. Blanche Dugdale to *The Times*, 14 December 1936.

However, the forces of cohesion on Balfour's list applied in different degrees to different dominions. Dutch Afrikaners, French Canadians, and the Irish did not cohere whole-heartedly through religion, race, or language, and had only a qualified 'pride in various manifestations' of the empire which had once conquered them. But we may add to Balfour's list the common defence system, at that date still based primarily upon the British navy; the network of financial interests controlled from the City of London; and the sharing of democratic principles and practices. Even so, in the event of any transition from formal to practical equality, such as must take place if and when the United Kingdom ceased to be regarded tacitly as the inevitable leader, centrifugal influences might be expected to be very strong in such an organization as this 'third British empire', now beginning to be called the 'British commonwealth of nations'. And so it proved.

We have already traced (p. 77) the stages by which the single unifying Crown became, first a number of crowns with the same wearer, and then the headship of a commonwealth in which some but not all the member states recognized the head as sovereign. We have also traced the evolution of the governor-generalship first into an office unrelated to the policy of the United Kingdom, and later into one which might even be unrelated to the outlook of the royal house. An important parallel development was that there ceased to be a single status of British subject, based on allegiance owed to one sovereign throughout the world-wide possessions of the crown. The status of 'British subject or Commonwealth citizen' continued to exist, but it gave no legal advantages to its possessor except what the law of a particular part of the Commonwealth might happen to confer. In the United Kingdom he still had freedom of entry and automatic rights of local citizenship, including the franchise and ability to sit in either house of parliament; in the Asiatic member states, on the other hand, commonwealth citizenship as such received no legal recognition, though some advantages over alien immigrants or visitors were conceded in practice. Thus the status of most account everywhere in the Commonwealth was the local one—'citizen of the United Kingdom and colonies', 'citizen of Canada', etc., for which each self-governing unit laid down its own conditions.

The legal side, as Balfour pointed out, matters least. Nevertheless, some significance attaches to the clauses of the statute of Westminster which, in freeing the dominions from the obligations of any British legislation—unless any dominion on any occasion requested otherwise—entitled them to alter their own constitutions, based on acts of the United Kingdom parliament. Canada has preferred to leave the delicately adjusted federal relationship between its central government and the ten provinces under the protection of the British North America Act, by which the federal system had originally been set up in 1867. But the Irish Free State, whose constitution derived from a treaty settlement approved by the United Kingdom parliament as recently as December 1921, used its freedom to ignore the treaty and enact a new constitution, derived from the 'will of the Irish people'. The right of appeal to the judicial committee of the privy council, the long-standing privilege of all overseas subjects of the crown, though retained by Australia and New Zealand and some newer member states, was likewise abolished by individual decisions elsewhere. Lastly, we must notice the disappointing results of the imperial economic conference held at Ottawa in 1932. The return of the United Kingdom to a tariff system after nearly a century of free trade seemed to some people to provide a golden opportunity to strengthen the bonds of empire with an imperial customs union, but no dominion except possibly New Zealand was disposed to limit its own industrial growth for the sake of imperial sentiment.

The second world war, fought in almost every part of the world, imposed a much more severe strain than its predecessor upon the unity of the Commonwealth. Eire, the former Irish Free State, remained neutral; the Union of South Africa joined in after a cabinet crisis and the defeat of an anti-war government by the perilously small majority of 80 to 67. Canada, Australia, and New Zealand came most devotedly to the rescue of Britain in the first disastrous phases of the long struggle, but those disasters also made it very clear that under modern conditions of war the safety of Canada depends primarily upon her great neighbour to the southward. In a more dramatic way the successes of the Japanese in 1941–2, when Singapore fell and the British navy was virtually withdrawn from Far Eastern waters, put Australia and New Zealand in a position of extreme peril, from which only the Americans could rescue them: the sequel after the war was the ANZUS treaty of 1951, by which the defence of the Pacific dominions became formally an American interest without British participation in the agreement. Meanwhile in India the advance of the Japanese, who swept through Burma and into Assam, had been regarded less as a reason for rallying either to Britain or to America for the sake of resistance to invasion than as welcome evidence that the ascendancy of the west was at an end. The same lesson was learnt in even harsher circumstances in Malaya, Burma, and Hong Kong.

Imperial Revolution

Accordingly, the years after the war witnessed the rapid establishment of practical alongside the old formal equality. Imperial conferences, which since their first inception at Queen Victoria's two jubilees had brought prime ministers to London for the regular discussion of common problems under the chairmanship of the British prime minister or secretary of state, fell into disuse. So did the very name of dominion, which was felt to imply some inferiority of status as compared with the United Kingdom: in 1947 the dominions office, which had been separated from the colonial office as recently as 1925, took on the name of commonwealth relations office, the relations being those with 'member states'. The right of secession, never mentioned in any of the documents of empire, was asserted by Burma in 1948, soon after its recovery from the Japanese, by Eire in 1949, and by the Sudan (an Anglo-Egyptian condominium) in 1956. In the case of the Irish Britain made the concession that citizens of the Irish republic may claim United Kingdom citizenship through residence in the same way as a citizen from a member state of the Commonwealth. But the most important change was probably that which concerned the 400,000,000 Indian subjects of the crown.

Within a month of the final enactment of the Indian Independence Act in July 1947, the government of the United Kingdom relinquished the control it had exercised over part and then the whole of India during a period of nearly two centuries. It was a control that had signified much in terms of prestige, economic gains, and military influence in the affairs of the east. Since no compromise had been able to reconcile Hindu and Mohammedan, two separate dominions were established. By far the larger of the two is India, which—as we have already seen (p. 78)—

decided almost immediately to adopt a republican constitution. The wheel had come full circle from Disraeli's proclamation of Queen Victoria as empress of India, when the Commonwealth Declaration of 28 April 1949 accorded continued membership of the Commonwealth to a republic of India in virtue of her 'acceptance of the king as the symbol of the free association of its independent member nations and as such the Head of the Commonwealth'. The same document quietly acknowledged the fact that the past cannot rule the future by dropping the adjective 'British' from the title of the multi-racial Commonwealth, and George VI with kingly tact addressed the assembly of prime ministers, one of whom was no longer 'his' minister, in terms of 'our Commonwealth', 'our brotherhood of nations'.

2. RELATIONS BETWEEN THE UNITED KINGDOM AND OTHER MEMBER STATES

The achievement of dominion status by India had been nearly complete before the war, and was unequivocally promised, together with the right to declare herself independent, by the Cripps mission in 1942. But as regards other parts of the empire it is safe to say that, although self-government was the declared goal of British rule, the rulers of 1939 still thought of it as a goal that lay far ahead and envisaged a form of self-government that would be consistent with the survival of a healthy and helpful British influence. Therefore the most striking feature of recent Commonwealth history has been the steady advance of the principal dependencies of the United Kingdom into the ranks of the member states. One reason has certainly been the very rapid rise of nationalist feeling among colonial peoples everywhere. A second is probably the successful precedent established in the case of India, where religious feuds and the absolutist tendencies of powerful native states were commonly expected to make a change of regime particularly hazardous. But a third undoubtedly is the skill which British administrators have for the most part shown in facilitating a peaceful transition and adapting themselves to new conditions, in which the former master could only stay on as the servant of an alien community. A prime minister of the United Kingdom put the British programme of liberation in its world setting when he said:

> The concept of an expanding Commonwealth in which peoples emerging from a dependent status become equal partners by their own free choice . . . may well prove to be one of the greatest developments in the course of human progress.[1]

The facts may be briefly stated. India and Pakistan prepared the way for their neighbour Ceylon, which was given the same independent status one year later almost without controversy. Both Pakistan and Ceylon subsequently followed India's lead by establishing republican constitutions. To these two additions were made in 1957. Ghana was the first member state composed of native African peoples, and in comparison with the Indians and Ceylonese these were peoples with no ancient civilization of their own dating from before the European conquest. The federation of Malaya was in two respects an even bolder experiment: the population was about equally divided between Malaysian and other elements, mainly Chinese,

[1] Mr. Harold Macmillan in a broadcast from New Zealand, 28 January 1958.

and in view of its basis in the ten Malay states it was allowed, as we have seen (p. 78), to have its own independent monarchy. In 1960 the single event of the achievement of independence by Nigeria reduced the population remaining in the dependencies of the United Kingdom by one-half. From the speed with which independent constitutions were then formulated for Tanganyika, the Federation of the West Indies, and other, smaller areas made it reasonable to conclude that, wherever a colony or group of colonies seemed capable of leading an independent existence, the opportunity for it would quickly be given.

Nevertheless, it must be acknowledged that this policy can only be adopted at the expense of white settler minorities and trading interests, which have always looked to the United Kingdom government for support. In principle, indeed, the matter had been settled as long ago as July 1923, when the first Baldwin government in the case of Kenya thought it necessary to record their considered opinion that the interests of the African natives must be paramount, and that if, and when, these interests and the interests of the immigrant races should conflict, the former should prevail.[1] But in Kenya in 1923 the primary reference was to Indian immigrants, and down to the war the implications of this doctrine of trusteeship in general made themselves only gradually felt. The wind of change having since then blown up to a hurricane, the hardships involved in carrying the programme of liberation to its logical conclusion now seem inescapable, both in east and in central Africa. It is significant that the determination of the government of the Union of South Africa to carry the opposite programme, that of *apartheid*,

[1] Kenya White Paper, Cmd. 1922, p. 9.

likewise to its logical conclusion precipitated a conflict in which that not unimportant member state was lost to the Commonwealth.

Apart from the monarchy and the office of governor-general, in so far as its occupant may still happen to be chosen from among distinguished figures in British public life, what are the institutions that still unite Britain with the other member states? The formal links are three. The *Commonwealth Relations Office* is a comparatively small government department dealing with government departments in the other member states; on major issues, however, messages pass direct between prime ministers. A high commissioner is sent to the capital of each member state, and similar *high commissioners* are sent by each of them to serve in London: their precedence is that of an ambassador and their duties are roughly similar. But at the policy-making level resort must be had to conferences, which are nowadays held at such times and places and with such participation and for such purposes as the member states of the Commonwealth find convenient. Separate meetings have been held among ministers of finance, defence, foreign affairs, and supply, but the most important and frequent have been the private and informal *meetings of prime ministers*. It is said that no votes are taken, but among the subjects on which unanimity is required is any proposal for the recognition of a new member state or of an old one on its transformation into a republic. Hence the crisis at the prime ministers' conference of 1961 (referred to above), when the expression of acute dissatisfaction with South African racial policy made it clear that the new South African Republic would not be acceptable as a member state pending some measure of reform. The South African government then terminated an association with the United Kingdom which under different forms had lasted continuously since 1806.

The Commonwealth is also closely linked by trade. Although rising prices have further reduced the importance of imperial preferences, in 1957 45 per cent of United Kingdom trade was with Commonwealth countries; in New Zealand the proportion was 73 per cent, and it fell below 30 per cent only in the case of Canada. Every member state except Canada is in the sterling area, established in September 1939 to conserve gold and dollar credits, and although some other countries are included, the area organization has always been under British and Commonwealth control. About 70 per cent of all external investment in the Commonwealth, apart from Canada, comes from Britain. A further sum of about £15,000,000 a year is made available through the Colombo plan as a British contribution to the development of the poorer countries of east Asia: neither contributors nor beneficiaries are confined to the Commonwealth, but it was the Commonwealth finance ministers that formulated the plan in 1950.

The organization of defence and the resulting commitments are, like the foreign policy on which they are based, the independent concern of every member state. This, however, is another matter in which the United Kingdom still generally takes the lead, since her expenditure in men and material is related to her widely scattered responsibilities. Some of the other member states provide special training facilities, as they did during the war: British airmen get flying practice in Canada, and atomic weapons made in the United Kingdom are tested in the Australian deserts. Officers from the United Kingdom also take part in courses at the Canadian and other staff colleges, and

Relations between the UK and Other Member States

there is a regular interchange of service liaison staffs. But the imperial defence college in London, the joint services staff college in Buckinghamshire, and the annual conference held by the chief of the imperial general staff, all of which are attended by officers from all parts of the Commonwealth, are probably the strongest influences towards the establishment of an agreed defence doctrine.

The first step towards agreement, whether in defence or any other aspect of policy, is a habit of consultation. Its extent has been carefully defined in the most recent authoritative study as follows:

> There is an obligation to communicate and consult.... The development of institutions of co-operation within the Commonwealth has... been determined by these principles, that communication and consultation must be made full and effective, but that no obligation to go beyond this point could be undertaken.[1]

What does this mean in practice?

There is much pooling of information and channelling of goodwill through various non-political institutions. These include the Commonwealth parliamentary association, dating from 1911; the economic committee, agricultural bureaux, and scientific offices; the shipping committee and air transport council; the association of universities of the British Commonwealth; and last but by no means least, the telecommunications board. For the availability of news of all kinds is an important factor in building up the interest and sympathy without which the modern Commonwealth cannot hope to survive: Reuters' London-based news agency, the overseas services of the

[1] K. C. Wheare: *The Constitutional Structure of the Commonwealth* (1960), p. 135.

BBC, and the dissemination of newspapers and periodicals from the United Kingdom therefore have a big part to play.

As regards the formulation of foreign policy through effective consultation, however, it would be dangerous to generalize. An increasing proportion of member states derive their traditions and way of life from sources which are predominantly non-British and even non-European. This is to some extent hidden at first because modes of government are still on the whole similar, being derived from the period of British ascendancy. But time may increase the centrifugal tendency, and just as there is no right of veto upon the actions of any member state, so we must assume that consultation will be restricted to what each member may continue to find convenient.

3. THE DEPENDENCIES

The dependencies of the United Kingdom at the present day are no more than a fragment of the colonial empire of the recent past. The main reason for this is, of course, the rapid forward movement which has carried the larger, wealthier, and more cohesive dependencies to a higher status within the Commonwealth. Another, much smaller group has chosen instead to sever the British connection altogether. A third group consists of dependencies of other member states, which though belonging to the Commonwealth have no direct connection with the United Kingdom. Thus eastern New Guinea has been administered by the government of Australia, western Samoa until recently by that of New Zealand, and South-West Africa by that of the former Union of South Africa.

The legal status of the dependencies varies greatly.

Some are *Trust Territories,* as was Tanganyika, a German colony captured during the first world war and administered first as a League of Nations 'mandate' and later as a United Nations 'trust'. The dependencies of other members of the Commonwealth are nearly all of this kind, but the Union government refused to admit that it was bound by any obligations of trusteeship regarding South-West Africa. A number of United Kingdom dependencies are *Protectorates,* countries which have not been annexed (so that their inhabitants are not technically British subjects) but which by treaty or in some other way have nevertheless come to accept the power and jurisdiction of the crown. Uganda, for example, derives its present status from the proclamation of a protectorate in 1894 over the native kingdom of Buganda and adjoining territories. In southern Africa there is a special regime applicable to the *High Commission Territories,* consisting of Basutoland, the Bechuanaland Protectorate, and Swaziland: these are controlled by resident commissioners acting on behalf of a high commissioner, who was also the United Kingdom high commissioner in the Union of South Africa and was responsible to the commonwealth relations office in both capacities. There are also some small *Protected States,* such as the Pacific island of Tonga, an independent kingdom except for British protection in its relations with foreign powers. One *Condominium* must be mentioned, the New Hebrides, which have been the joint responsibility of Britain and France since 1906, and there are certain *Leased Territories* which form a temporary addition to the mainland possessions of Hong Kong. But of the numerous administrative units concerned, the majority have the status of *Colonies,* to which subordinate dependencies may also be attached, as are the 300 inhabitants of Tristan da

o

Cunha to the colony of St. Helena, though 1,700 miles away.

These colonies were variously acquired by right of discovery, settlement, conquest, or voluntary cession, and the recognized dates of acquisition range between 1624, when Barbados (now in the Federation) first passed into English hands, and 1946, when its last British rajah ceded Sarawak to the crown. Their internal administration nevertheless follows a common pattern, except that a trust territory has its interests safeguarded by the United Nations, standing as it were behind parliament and the colonial office (see p. 218). The governor is the direct representative of the crown, with powers defined by letters patent under the great seal and by supplementary instructions. Since these instruments also define the powers of other officials and the council or councils, they are equivalent to a constitution for the colony—an arrangement which facilitates local variation and necessary modification. The governor has under him a colonial secretary, chief justice, and other heads of departments (finance, public health, education, police, etc.) who normally form the nucleus of his Executive Council, to which other persons may be appointed by nomination—or election.

But it is in the changing composition of the Legislative Council that the stages in the advance towards full self-government are usually most clearly to be seen. To begin with, the majority of its members may be officials and the others nominees of the governor. An elected element is then added, and this may be based at first on a very narrow franchise. With the growth of political experience in the colony more people are given the vote, and their elected representatives come to form a majority and finally the whole of the legislative council. Once it is established that

The Dependencies

the legislative council is a truly representative body, it earns the right to appoint some of its members to seats in the executive council, from which the nominated members and eventually even the officials are withdrawn. The executive council thus becomes a cabinet of ministers, and only the existence of reserve powers, entitling the governor to disallow legislation or to disregard the wishes of either council in an emergency, then stands between the colony and the achievement of independent status.

Nevertheless, it is possible to place too much emphasis upon the western idea of the franchise. Some of the most successful work in colonial administration has been done through the system of Indirect Rule, whereby the existing institutions of native tribes and communities have been allowed to continue as the basis of government—for tax collection, the judicial work, and the control of public services—with only a limited amount of advice and supervision from British officials. Lord Lugard, who became the first governor-general of Nigeria, was the foremost of the pioneers who introduced this where native institutions were strong, partly to avoid friction and to reduce expenditure: but it is not only in Nigeria that rapid progress has been achieved by building upon ways of life which are wholly distinct from the European. It is also noteworthy that, in many places where self-government has been developed upon the European basis of the ballot-box, it has been necessary to have indirect elections, in which the voters choose representatives who choose the actual legislators, or to arrange for racial or religious communities to be the units represented rather than single-member geographical constituencies as in Britain.

The final authority over any dependency is parliament, which normally acts through the cabinet and the colonial office, while major questions, such as a transfer to independent status, are debated and voted upon by the two houses. The day-to-day business dealt with by the colonial office includes the appointment of governors and other officials, down to the district commissioners, who deal directly with the affairs of a relatively small area. Besides its control of recruitment and careers, the colonial office also has direct contact with individual officers through the regulation which entitles any person in a colony to petition the secretary of state through the governor, who is bound to transmit each such petition with his comments. The judiciary is subject to the colonial office as regards appointments, but its independent status is helped by the fact that in certain cases an appeal lies from the supreme court of any colony to the judicial committee of the privy council. Lastly, we may notice that the governor of a colony is also its commander-in-chief: in Jamaica he even retained the ancient Spanish title of captain-general. But where there are local military forces they are administered by the colonial office and serve primarily to maintain good order within the colony. External defence is in any case a responsibility borne by the United Kingdom.

The notion of empire as power dies hard, though at the present day fortress colonies such as Gibraltar, Malta, and Aden might prove more of a liability than an asset in the defence of those areas of the earth's surface for which the government of the United Kingdom still bears the primary responsibility. Equally persistent is the notion that empire means wealth, although no dependency has subsidized the British budget since the Stamp Act was repealed, just too late to placate the Americans, in 1766. On the contrary, Britain is committed to an annual expenditure of nearly £20,000,000 under the Colonial Development and Welfare Acts, and about as much again is spent in grants to colonies for specific purposes. Nor does trade provide a very substantial compensation: about a third of the imports of the colonies are from the United Kingdom, which in return takes about one-quarter of their exports. Since 1948 a Colonial Development Corporation, with power to borrow more than £100,000,000, has been trying to increase their productive capacity. Thus it is right to regard the dependencies as primarily a relic from the earlier stages of British history, which it is now the accepted policy to convert as quickly as possible into independent members of the Commonwealth.

XV

BRITAIN AND INTERNATIONAL INSTITUTIONS

1. BEFORE THE SECOND WORLD WAR

THE oldest international organization on a world-wide basis is the postal union, which since the 1870s has maintained a system of uniform charges and facilities for the exchange of correspondence among all civilized peoples. The frontier of the postal union is in a sense the world frontier of civilization. Nevertheless, its problems and the restrictions on national sovereignty which it imposes are, comparatively speaking, so trivial that we must look elsewhere for the true beginnings of international *political* organization. They are to be found in the concert of Europe, that practice of mutual consultation among the great powers which was inaugurated in 1815 and, although it failed to prevent the major wars of 1848-78, was for nearly forty years before 1914 a very real bulwark of peace. In 1898, for example, the powers established an international force to keep order in Crete, then a European danger-point, and in 1912-13 their ambassadors in London contrived to smooth over all the difficulties created by the aggrandizement of rival Balkan states in their war against Turkey, more than one of which might have produced a general European conflict.

The concert failed, indeed, to prevent the war of 1914,

but its history did not end there. In 1919 the council of the league of nations might have replaced it as the meeting-ground of the great powers of Europe and of two new-comers, the United States and Japan, which before the war had taken part in their deliberations on a few occasions only. But apart altogether from the refusal of the United States to join the league, the attempt to replace the concert broke down because the drafters of the league covenant included in the council some elected representatives of the smaller states, whose number steadily grew. Accordingly, the concert was revived. At first it was the allied powers of the war period which deliberated apart from the rest; then Germany claimed to be included, and finally Soviet Russia. Thus it came about that, in the succession of crises which Germany fomented in the years immediately preceding the war of 1939, the negotiations for her appeasement were conducted mainly through the foreign offices and embassies in the principal European capitals.

But the league of nations, though slighted by the great powers, has a lasting importance because it introduced the idea of world government. On the political side, the league was embodied in three main instruments. The first was the annual assembly at Geneva, to which some fifty-four sovereign states (about three-quarters of the world) sent representatives. On some occasions a new law or convention might be drafted by the assembly, though the law came into force only in so far as it was ratified by the various governments—usually a slow process. But to quote the opinion of an expert observer at the time:

> By far the most important function of the Assembly is to provide a forum for the discussion of world affairs. The general debate which takes place during the first week provides a unique occasion, such as was nowhere available under

the pre-war system, for the expression of the opinions and conscience of the peoples represented there. During that week in September Geneva is the best sounding-board in the world. . . . The net result is always both instructive and inspiring.[1]

In other words, the league assembly focused and strengthened whatever forces were making for goodwill in the world: but it did not manage to crush their opposites.

Much the same may be said of the council, which was meant to function as a cabinet. In the council, as in the assembly, important decisions had to be unanimous, except for the actual parties to a dispute. But once this obstacle was surmounted, the council was in a position to deal with international difficulties of any kind by methods of practical adjustment, while legal disputes could be determined by another league organ, the permanent court of international justice, whose jurisdiction Britain in 1929 accepted as compulsory. If all else failed, the league had in theory agreed methods of dealing with an aggressor by imposing sanctions, such as an economic blockade. All that was lacking was the will to banish war.

In the long run the world services came to constitute the most hopeful side of the league's activities. International communications, economic and financial co-operation, and public health—including the suppression of drug and other unsavoury traffics—were all watched and safeguarded by committees of experts, under the supervision of the league secretariat at Geneva. This first international civil service was, indeed, responsible in one way or another for many of the league's more solid achievements. Finally, there was a parallel organization, known as

[1] Sir Alfred Zimmern: *The League of Nations and the Rule of Law* (1936), p. 465.

the international labour office, which watched industrial conditions and had as its main task the gradual levelling-up of wages and hours to the standard of the more advanced nations, receiving powerful support from the United States, which joined in this part of the league's work as a full member.

However, the general prestige of the league declined rapidly with its failure to curb Japanese aggression in 1932 or Italian aggression in 1935, though it was left for the second world war to deal the final blow. In December 1939 its authority was invoked for the last time to condemn the Russian invasion of Finland. Within twelve months Germany had overrun the continent so completely that in Europe at least the league had lost all significance; and when the later fortunes of the war joined Russia with the western allies there was every reason for the decision to found world order upon a new basis. But since the new world organization was not to be centred upon Europe, we may consider first the new institutions by which Britain is now linked with her more immediate neighbours.

2. THE NEW EUROPE

The second world war brought Britain into closer relations with Continental states than she had known since the middle ages. In June 1940 Churchill as prime minister offered the French a common citizenship with the British in the vain hope of keeping them in the war. For several momentous years London was the home of the exiled governments of free Europe. Then came the campaigns of liberation, which gave new meaning to ideas of European unity. Finally, there was the gradual realization that together Britain, France, and the rest of western Europe now carried only the weight of a single lesser force in comparison with the two world forces, the United States and the Soviet Union. Moreover, Europe emerged from the war not only terribly weakened but divided ideologically between east and west. For the western half, therefore, the urge to unite was now a natural reaction to the Communist threat and the American promise: for in American eyes a Europe that could recognize the need to sink its differences, as the thirteen ex-British colonies had done when they made the American constitution, was more deserving of help than one that clung to its outmoded separate sovereignties.

Accordingly, a whole series of European organizations sprang up, which—subject only to trade interests—enjoyed a high degree of American (and Canadian) support. The British response was more positive than in the days of insular security: otherwise this subject could find no place in a discussion of British institutions. But her ties with the other member states of the Commonwealth; her specially intimate, separate relationship with the United States, which the circumstances of the war and the genius of Churchill had strengthened; and also perhaps some lack of confidence regarding her own economic vigour, a fear that she might not long remain the senior partner in a new firm—all these prevented Britain from travelling very far or very fast along the road to a united Europe. Practical commitments for clearly defined objects were fairly readily accepted, and the general principle of interdependence with other western powers had the approval of all political parties except the Communist: but there was still strong resistance to plans for federation or any other derogation from the independent sovereignty of the United Kingdom.

In the 1950s Britain's commitments under the *North Atlantic Treaty* of 4 April 1949 clearly ranked first. This pledged its twelve original members to meet armed attack

> by taking forthwith, individually and in concert with the other Parties, such action as it deems necessary, including the use of armed force to restore and maintain the security of the North Atlantic area (Article 5)

and in addition

> by means of continuous and effective self-help and mutual aid, to maintain and develop their individual and collective capacity to resist armed attack.

These clauses constituted the main defence of the free world against piecemeal Soviet aggression in the west, especially after the inclusion of Greece and Turkey in 1952 and of the German Federal Republic in 1955. Nevertheless, the regional defence of western Europe was given greater precision by forming the *Western European Union*, based on Britain's post-war military treaties with France and the Low Countries, to which Italy and the German Federal Republic were invited to adhere in 1954. The institutions of the Union include a council of ambassadors or foreign ministers and a consultative assembly of parliamentarians from the member countries, serving chiefly as a means of ventilating regional military problems.

The organs of NATO are of much greater importance, because it is through them that the severely limited resources of western Europe have become effectively linked with those of the United States and Canada. NATO was provided with a Council, composed of ministers and their permanent deputies from the countries concerned, and with a highly influential secretary-general. Since both political and economic collaboration were envisaged as taking place under NATO auspices, conferences of parliamentarians were also introduced. But the military structure remained the element of paramount importance, for which Britain even sacrificed a portion of its cherished sovereignty. In theory the military policy of NATO was to be determined by the council and implemented by two bodies of experts—the military committee, composed of chiefs of staff or their representatives from all member countries, and their Standing Group at Washington, in which the chiefs of staff represented were to be the American, British, French, and one other chosen by rotation. In practice, however, the Supreme Allied Commander, Europe, who was always an American general, had the direct responsibility for the defence of the threatened European areas, as had the Supreme Atlantic Commander for protecting the vital sea lanes. In peacetime the latter commanded national forces for training purposes only, but the former had forces permanently assigned to him by the member states. There was also a very important peacetime development of installations such as airfields and radar networks for the benefit of NATO forces. The cost of this 'common infrastructure', of which America paid the lion's share, totalled about £700,000,000 in the first seven years.

In the event of aggression against the territory of a member state, NATO provided an inter-allied command structure already in being. The equipment and training of national forces were increasingly based on their eventual total subordination to that command. There was an agreed strategic doctrine of 'sword and shield', the sword of a nuclear counter-offensive and the shield of a previously prepared defence of land and sea areas with conventional and lesser nuclear weapons. But it is difficult to resist the conclusion that, in a major emergency, the fateful decision to make unlimited war might have to be taken without any effective consultation among the so-called sovereign states that signed the North Atlantic Treaty.

Almost in the same month as NATO, an ambitious political organization was set up, with a membership of fifteen European states. This was to function through an executive committee of ministers, a consultative annual assembly of parliamentarians, and a vigorous international secretariat based at its headquarters in Strasbourg. The name, *Council of Europe*, was a programme in itself; the non-military activities of the existing Western European Union were completely overshadowed; and the council quickly became involved in the projection of a European culture. As a political body, however, it made slow progress, since the ministers delegated by some of the member states—including Britain—were much more concerned to safeguard state sovereignty than to attempt to implement proposals made by enthusiasts in the assembly, which they treated as a mere debating society. One important exception was a convention for the protection of human rights and fundamental freedoms, based on the bitter experiences of the two preceding decades: this was duly ratified by almost every government concerned.

If vague political yearnings produced only rather ineffective political institutions, the economic plight of postwar Europe, no less than the Russian military threat, produced relatively efficient economic institutions. It was in connection with these that Britain adopted to some extent, as we shall see, a policy of formal abstention from membership. The beginning, indeed, was a period, now too readily forgotten, when western Europe could not have been saved by its own efforts, however complete and wholehearted the co-operation of Britain. In September 1947 the foreign secretary, Ernest Bevin, described the situation to the TUC in the following terms:

> This is the first time in British history for 400 years when Britain has been able to do nothing, either with goods or with money or with coal. My position as foreign secretary has been that for two years I have not had a single vote of credit in the House of Commons to assist in the rehabilitation work overseas. . . . Give me the tools of production and a full result and I will change the foreign policy of Europe and help in its rehabilitation. I cannot do it empty-handed.[1]

It was left therefore to the American Marshall Plan to 'change the foreign policy of Europe'—in other words, to stave off the advance of Communist revolution—by generous measures of first-aid. That aid was administered during four critical years (1948-52) by the *Organization for European Economic Co-operation*, representing the 17 western states which accepted the American offer—it was refused by the Communist states of eastern Europe—and from the outset the functions of the Organization included the development of economic co-operation among the members; since December 1960 they have further pledged themselves to the economic assistance of underdeveloped countries outside Europe. With all this work Britain, which had been a major beneficiary of the original Marshall Plan, has been closely associated: such co-operation involves no loss of sovereign control over her own affairs.

OECD, as it is now styled—the Organization for Economic Co-operation and Development—has four important organs. It is headed by a council, composed of

[1] Speech reported in *The Times*, 4 September 1947.

ministers or officials representing every member state, whose decisions must be unanimous if they are to take effect, and there is an executive committee of 11, which includes representatives of the United States and Canada. Technical committees, in which again every member is represented, play a big part, as does the secretariat in Paris, made up of about 200 'European civil servants' of a status equivalent to that of the administrative class in Britain. The British delegation to the Organization, working in Paris, is drawn normally from the staffs of the Treasury, Board of Trade, and Foreign Office, which gives some indication of the scope of the permanent activities. As OEEC, it was particularly concerned with monetary agreements, the reduction of trade restrictions, intra-European investment, the easing of raw material shortages, and the increase of productivity (including, for instance, some pioneer projects in the field of nuclear energy). A good many agreements have been successfully negotiated, and even when insistence on national rights has prevented full success, the process of negotiation has often created a new awareness of, and some consideration for, specifically European interests.

Britain, however, refused to go further, when six powers—France, the German Federal Republic, Italy, Belgium, Holland, and Luxemburg—began to develop a *European Economic Community* of a supra-national character. The first step was taken in 1951, when coal, iron, and steel were placed under a High Authority located at Luxemburg. Six years later two more treaties set up a similar authority to undertake all development of nuclear power, except for specifically military requirements, and to establish a common market. With the first two of these far-reaching projects Britain became very loosely linked through a delegation. But in face of the common market set up by the treaty of Rome, with its strong political basis, Britain began to organize a very much smaller *European Free Trade Association* among seven of the remaining west European powers. This came into operation in May 1960 under the terms of the treaty of Stockholm, which provided for a progressive reduction of all tariffs and the abolition of those on industrial products within ten years.

The *Common Market*, however, succeeded beyond (British) expectation. In the summer of 1961, therefore, the United Kingdom was belatedly entering upon a difficult period of re-appraisal. The claims of Commonwealth exporters, the vested interests of British farmers, and the insular prejudice against surrendering any fraction of political control to a continental organization all barred the way. But to obtain entry to the Common Market was now judged by ministers to be necessary—and necessity is the mother of invention.

3. WORLD ORGANIZATION

Since the first atomic bombs were dropped on Japanese cities in the last phase of the war, the achievement of a world order has been central to the hopes of every human being who realizes that a third world war would almost certainly destroy civilization and might destroy mankind. But for the British a world order has additional attractions: our island presents a particularly vulnerable target for the warfare of to-morrow; our decline in total and still more in relative strength means that we can no longer even dream of controlling world developments through the influence enjoyed by the strong; and at the same time the degree of success achieved by the Commonwealth experiment suggests that in a well-organized world order Britain might still have a very effective part to play. A study of British institutions of to-day may therefore end with some consideration of the growth of UN.

At the outset hopes ran very high. After the charter of the united nations had been formally adopted by 51 states at the San Francisco conference in June 1945 the first assembly was convened in London the following January. At that date the British government's intention, stated in a parliamentary answer, was 'to work the institutions of the United Nations in such a way that in due course we shall see produced the equivalent of world government'. However, disappointment quickly followed, as the rift opened between east and west, as naked displays of force replaced rational argument, and as the exclusion of communist China (against the wishes of Britain) was increasingly seen to justify the very criticism that had been levied against the league of nations—that a world force was absent from the counsels of the world. The effect on British opinion can be measured by the fact that the united nations association, which was founded to sustain interest in the new organization, mustered only 70,000 members, as compared with nearly 1,000,000 in the league of nations association at its zenith a generation earlier. In 1956, in particular, the limits of the authority of the united nations were forcibly brought home to British people by the utter helplessness of world opinion in face of Russia's brutal repression of the Hungarian bid for freedom. But disappointment over the fact that the world powers are still a law unto themselves must not be allowed to hide the important field of activity which the organs of the united nations nevertheless provide for Britain.

As one of the five permanent members of the *Security Council*, the United Kingdom is brought into direct relations with Soviet Russia in circumstances which from time to time allow her to play the part of a mediator. Little more can be achieved there by any power, since except in matters of procedure the security council can take no action without the approval of all five permanent members and two of the six others. In the *General Assembly*, on the other hand, Britain is a participant in annual sessions which are based upon the sovereign equality of a hundred member states. The debates at their best may express something like the conscience of mankind; at their worst they serve only to exacerbate international relations, as world publicity may tempt the strong to attempt intimidation and certainly tempts the weak to seize their chance of wordy defiance. But among the advantages of the assembly must be included the opportunity it gives for private meetings of Commonwealth representatives, where compromise solutions for problems that divide the Commonwealth as well as the rest of the world can sometimes be worked out in an atmosphere of mutual confidence.

The *International Court of Justice* at The Hague, which is an almost exact replica of the permanent court set up under league auspices, has had the full support of the United Kingdom. The two most recent British members of the court of 15 judges—who are nominated by national groups but require for their election an absolute majority in the assembly and in the security council—have both of them held the chair of international law at Cambridge. Britain has brought cases before the court, and has also figured as defendant; as they must be actions between states and normally such as involve questions of international law, the principal British reservation concerns disputes within the Commonwealth. But our first major suit, when Albania had sunk two British destroyers in the Corfu channel, illustrates the limits of the court's authority, for the Albanian government, though accepting the jurisdiction of the court, has paid no part of the damages awarded.

The *Economic and Social Council*, on the other hand, was a new venture, designed in the halcyon days of 1945 for a more prominent role than even the security council, in the belief that it would promote broad advances in status and standard of living which should cause all prospects of international conflict to recede. Its 18 members, who meet twice a year for about a month at a time, are elected by the assembly, but Britain, as well as the greater powers, has always been included. But since the united nations has no power to legislate in economic and social matters, the council's main business is the creation of a progressive world opinion—a slow business, and one which Britain has been disposed to decry as over-expensive. The detailed work is done by specialized agencies (mentioned below), but the council provides much technical information and advice; it is also responsible for the *Economic Council for Europe*, important because the east European countries participate, and for half a dozen relief funds, including UNICEF. The *Secretariat* must be mentioned because it is as completely international an institution as human nature permits. The first two secretary-generals have been a Norwegian and a Swede, having under them five assistants who are in effect nominated by the five main powers. Below this level the staff of about 4,000 officials—as compared with 600 in NATO or in OECD—is chosen from different nationalities in proportion to their contribution to the united nations budget.

UN has a further twofold relationship with the United Kingdom as a state which controls both dependencies in the ordinary sense and territories formerly administered as mandates of the league of nations. As regards the latter, a more effective supervision than that of the league's mandates commission is now exercised by the *Trusteeship Council*, of which the membership is evenly divided between those states which have, and others which have not, control of such territories. Reports are required by the council, which can receive petitions, hear complainants in person, and pay visits of inspection to the territory. Trusts have moved rapidly towards independence, but Nauru—a Pacific phosphate mine with a population of 4,000, of whom only half are native islanders—may be cited as an example of some trusts which cannot easily be dispensed with in the near future. As for dependencies, the united nations charter lists the duties involved in their control, notably the obligation to develop self-government, and calls upon the controlling power to furnish progress reports. In addition, the assembly has established a *Special Committee for Information*, composed in the same way as the trusteeship council, which has greatly extended the range of subjects on which reports are collected and studied. In 1958 there were 38 territories for which the United Kingdom was asked to furnish information, whereas the trust territories at that date were only three—Tanganyika, part of the Cameroons, and (jointly with Australia and New Zealand) the island of Nauru.

The united nations also operates through a number of *Specialized Agencies*. We can do no more than name the chief of these, since their work, which is mainly of an economic or social character, is for the most part concerned with backward countries and affects the United

Kingdom largely through the reports from dependencies, already mentioned. The ILO seeks to improve conditions in industry, the FAO in agriculture, and the WHO in the sphere of health. Several organizations also exist to help the growth of world trade. Lastly, reference must be made to UNESCO, for the idea of an educational, scientific, and cultural organization germinated in wartime London, where governments and scholars in exile saw in intellectual collaboration the hope of the future. Its constitution opens with lord Attlee's memorable words: 'Since wars begin in the minds of men, it is in the minds of men that the defences of peace must be constructed.' Accordingly, UNESCO seeks to spread education and to discourage national bias; to apply science to the needs of humanity, for instance in the reduction of desert areas and the production of more food from the ocean; and to stimulate cultural developments and interchanges. Translations from 25 languages, a trilingual library in New Delhi, recordings of folk music, and travelling art exhibitions are examples of what was being achieved by 1956 on an annual budget of only £11,000,000.

Given a satisfactory measure of political success, the general potentialities of UN are enormous. It could gather strength from the proliferation of non-governmental institutions with an international scope, which is a feature of the life of our age. By 1955 they had reached a total of about 1,200, and many of them, such as the world council of churches, the world federation of trade unions, or the inter-parliamentary union, tended to create world loyalties. There were also large regional groupings expressly provided for in the charter, including NATO and its eastern counterpart SEATO, which since 1954 has involved the United Kingdom and other member states of the Commonwealth with the United States and France in the collective defence of south-east Asia. But regional groupings may serve to divide as much as to unite. A more promising sign of the times is the attempt to link individuals rather than states by devising world-wide protection for human rights. A universal declaration of human rights was accepted by 48 members at the united nations assembly of 1948, and has since become established through the European convention which provides for a tribunal of human rights. The values to be safeguarded in this way range widely between the right to live (measures against slavery, torture, etc.) and the right to a livelihood, including provision for leisure and social security. Thus the ideas of freedom and welfare, which we saw in our first chapter to be characteristic of British institutions to-day, may come to characterize the world institutions of a brighter tomorrow.

DATES OF STATUTES AND OTHER MAIN EVENTS

1066   Norman conquest of England
1215   Magna Carta accepted by king John
1295   the 'model parliament' of Edward I
1536   incorporation of Wales in parliament (first act of union)
1559   act of supremacy (1 Eliz. I c. 1)
1598   poor law (overseers to levy rate)
1628   petition of right
1689   mutiny act; toleration act; bill of rights
1701   act of settlement
1704   Scottish act for securing the Protestant religion
1707   act of union with Scotland
1801   act of union with Ireland
1829   first metropolitan police establishment of 825 men
1832   great reform act
1833   first four factory inspectors appointed
1834   poor law amendment act (unions and boards of guardians)
1835   municipal corporations act
1839   Durham report (leading to responsible government in colonies)
1846   small debts act (county courts)
1867   British North America act; parliamentary reform act (Disraeli)
1868   trades union congress (first recognized meeting, at Manchester)

1869	charity organization society founded (later named the family welfare association)
1870	education act (Forster); civil service competitive examinations established by order in council
1871	local government board formed
1872	ballot act
1873	judicature act (supreme court of judicature established)
1875	public health act; artisans' dwellings act
1876	royal titles act (queen became empress of India)
1881	closure introduced in the house of commons
1884	parliamentary reform act (Gladstone)
1885	redistribution act (single-member constituencies)
1887	queen Victoria's golden jubilee; first colonial conference
1888	local government act (county councils)
1890	housing of the working classes act
1894	local government act (district councils)
1899	London government act (metropolitan boroughs)
1902	education act (Balfour)
1903	Letchworth founded (first garden city); beginning of Emmeline Pankhurst's women's social and political union (suffrage agitation)
1904	committee of imperial defence formally established, with the prime minister as the only permanent member
1906	trade disputes act (privileged status for trade unions)
1908	old age pensions act; port of London authority act
1911	parliament act; insurance act
1916	department of scientific and industrial research established
1918	representation of the people act; education act (Fisher)
1919	ministry of health set up; sex disqualification (removal) act
1920	disestablishment of the Anglican church in Wales by amended version of act of 1914; government of Ireland act (constitution of Northern Ireland)
1921	Irish free state treaty signed (December)

Dates of Statutes and Other Main Events

1924 housing act (Wheatley)
1925 widows' and orphans' pensions act
1926 general strike (May); first BBC charter
1928 equal franchise act
1929 local government act (boards of guardians abolished)
1931 statute of Westminster
1935 government of India act
1937 regency act
1939 militia act (April)
1940 colonial development and welfare act
1942 publication of Beveridge's *Report on Social Insurance and the Allied Services*
1944 education act (Butler)
1945 family allowances act
1946 Bank of England nationalized
1947 coal industry nationalized; commonwealth relations office established; Indian independence act (came into effect August 15); town and country planning act
1948 nationalization of transport and electricity supply; national assistance act; Ceylon became independent
1949 declaration of London (title of Head of Commonwealth introduced); second parliament act; nationalization of gas supply
1950 republican constitution established in India (January)
1951 ministry of housing and local government set up
1952 accession of queen Elizabeth II (February)
1954 atomic energy authority established
1957 independence of Ghana and the federation of Malaya
1958 life peerages act
1960 independence of Nigeria
1961 South African republic established, outside the Commonwealth; independence of Tanganyika and other states within the Commonwealth

NOTES AND DEFINITIONS

ACT OF SETTLEMENT: the statute of 1701, passed after the death of Anne's only surviving child, which gave the eventual succession to the throne to the nearest Protestant heir, the electress Sophia of Hanover, and her heirs; the *Legitimist Calendar* in 1910 calculated that this act and the bill of rights had deprived 1,000 persons then living of a claim to the British throne; the same law provided for the independence of judges after Anne's death.

ADOPTIVE ACTS: certain powers are made available to local authorities by general legislation, which they are free to adopt or not, as they please; library acts from 1850 to 1919 (inclusive) were all of this character; but the modern practice is to include permissive powers in a general act, e.g. the authorization of expenditure on various forms of entertainment by the local government act of 1948 (s. 132).

BILL OF RIGHTS: the statute enacted in December 1689, based upon the limitations of royal prerogative and other statements of constitutional principle which were contained in the declaration of rights; the latter document was accepted by William and Mary on 13 February immediately before they were proclaimed king and queen.

BRITISH NORTH AMERICA ACT: the statute of 1867 by which Canada (redivided into Quebec and Ontario), Nova Scotia, and New Brunswick formed the nucleus of the dominion of Canada under governor-general, nominated senate, and elective house of commons, with subordinate

Notes and Definitions

lieutenant-governors and legislatures of provinces; the name 'dominion' was preferred to 'kingdom' because the colonial office feared to offend Americans, and is plausibly derived from Psalm 72: 8 or Zechariah 9: 10.

BY-LAWS: regulations made by local authorities or public corporations under act of parliament; penalties for breaches must be fines of a limited amount; local government by-laws require approval from the appropriate government department, and by-laws can also be disallowed by the courts as being either *ultra vires* or unreasonable.

CITY: according to Coke and Blackstone, a corporate town which is or has been the seat of a bishop; some that lost their bishop have also lost the distinctive title and, more important, it has been conferred by letters patent in modern times on other large or otherwise specially distinguished towns (e.g. Birmingham 1889, Leeds 1893, Westminster 1900, Cambridge 1951).

CIVIL LIST: annual payments to the sovereign, fixed by statute at the beginning of a reign and charged upon the consolidated fund, to defray expenses of the household, privy purse, royal bounty, etc.; the total of £475,000 is much smaller than the hereditary revenues from crown lands, etc., which the sovereign surrenders to parliament.

COMMON LAW: law common to the whole realm which has found expression, not in statutes but in the expositions and decisions of judges in the higher courts, and is therefore based largely on precedents; its principles are also invoked by modern judges to help in the interpretation of statute law.

COMPTROLLER AND AUDITOR-GENERAL: an official with the same security of tenure as a judge, appointed since 1866 with two functions: (*a*) to authorize payments to the treasury from the consolidated fund after satisfying himself that they have parliamentary approval; (*b*) to examine the accounts of departments and report unauthorized or extravagant expenditure to the public accounts committee of the house of commons.

CONSOLIDATED FUND: instituted by the younger Pitt in 1787 as the account at the Bank of England into which all revenue and proceeds of public loans are paid and from which all government expenditure is drawn; consolidated fund services are items of expenditure (e.g. civil list) which can be drawn from the fund without any annual authorization by parliament.

CONVENTIONS OF THE CONSTITUTION: accepted practices to which sovereign, cabinet, and parliament regularly adhere, but which are not laid down by law; the growth of tradition is a factor in securing their observance, but in most cases any breach can be seen to involve grave political difficulties; that the royal assent to legislation is never withheld is a clear example.

CORONER: an official elected by the freeholders of each county as early as 1194 to safeguard crown interests, which have dwindled to the holding of inquests regarding cases of sudden death (which may involve the queen's peace) and treasure trove (finds of gold and silver belong to the crown, though they are customarily returned to the finder); now a local government appointment.

DURHAM REPORT: a 300-page document laid before parliament in January 1839 after lord Durham's resignation of his post as governor-general and high commissioner in Canada; it advocated that the executive council should be responsible to the Canadian legislature; responsible government was granted to Nova Scotia in 1846 and to Canada in 1848, when the governor-general was Durham's son-in-law, lord Elgin.

GREAT REFORM ACT: so called because the reform of the franchise in 1832 was a fundamental constitutional change which made the later franchise reforms readily acceptable;

the immediate increase of voters in Great Britain was from 439,970 to 717,254; the act of 1867 raised the immediate total to 2,230,795 and that of 1884 to 4,931,371; as a percentage of male population the growth was from 5·6 to 8·8, 18·3, and 32·7 respectively.

HABEAS CORPUS: this important safeguard of the liberty of the subject is said to rest upon common law declared by Magna Carta; it was strengthened in 1641 (against the prerogative courts), 1679 (for all criminal charges), and 1816 (in some other cases); the last period of its suspension by parliament terminated in 1818.

LORD CHANCELLOR: the lord high chancellor of England as keeper of the great seal was once chief minister and still presides over the house of lords by right (i.e. even if a commoner); he presides in the two highest courts and exercises judicial patronage, down to the appointment of J.P.s, for which he is not directly responsible to the cabinet; the office may not be held by a Roman Catholic.

MANDAMUS: an order from the queen's bench division of the high court, issued where a complainant has no other means of compelling a public authority to carry out a duty which it owes to him; it can be used against government departments as well as lower courts of law, local authorities, and public utility undertakings, provided that the duty apparently neglected would be owing to the individual and not merely to the crown.

MARTIAL LAW: law imposed by the military upon civilians, against which the petition of right protested in 1628, has not been experienced in England since the civil war; it would be authorized by common law if strictly necessary to safeguard the peace and independence of the realm, and in 1940 the treachery act empowered the attorney-general to allow enemy aliens to be tried by court-martial; but an emergency powers act (No. 2, 1940) provided for war zone courts to make recourse to martial law less necessary in the event of an invasion.

NATURAL JUSTICE: rules used by judges in determining the validity of procedure used by administrative tribunals, such as the duty of hearing both sides to a dispute and that a man shall not be judge in his own cause.

ORDER IN COUNCIL: an executive order approved by the sovereign at a formal meeting of the privy council, which may be based either upon the royal prerogative (e.g. orders for the summoning, prorogation, and dissolution of parliament) or upon acts of parliament providing for the issue of such orders (e.g. special constables act, 1914, s. 1 (1), 'His Majesty may, by order in council, make regulations with respect to the appointment and position of special constables . . .').

PARLIAMENT ACT: the act of 1911, a sequel to the lords' rejection of the 1909 budget, was regarded as a major constitutional change; it was passed by the house of lords in view of king George V's promise to create peers, which some Conservatives claimed would not have been given by a more experienced monarch; its powers have been used to enact the Irish home rule bill (1914), the Welsh church disestablishment bill (1914), and the second parliament bill (1949).

PETITION: the right of subjects to petition the crown was protected by the bill of rights (1689), but petitions to parliament, presented by a member of either house (or the sheriffs of London) have latterly been more important; in the commons they are referred to a select committee, which may have them printed for circulation, but are not normally debated.

PETITION OF RIGHT: statute of 1628 declaring the illegality of unparliamentary taxation, arbitrary imprisonment, forced billeting, and martial law; this was the first statutory restriction of the powers of the crown since the accession of the Tudors (1485).

POLICE FORCES: petty or parish constables, from whom the modern police constable derives some of his powers, were instituted in 1285; the appointment of special constables by justices of the peace in emergency was regularized by statute in 1673; boroughs were required to provide police forces in 1835, but for counties they were an optional provision from 1839 to 1856; in 1947 the police forces of non-county boroughs were merged in their county forces.

PRIVATE BILLS: bills concerning the interests of individuals or corporate bodies are proposed and opposed by lawyers licensed to act as parliamentary agents; the main examination in either house is made by a very small committee, which hears counsel and witnesses, but such bills must pass through all the same formal stages as a public bill, their special character is shown by the wording of the royal assent, *Soit fait comme il est désiré*.

PRIVILEGES OF PARLIAMENT: besides freedom of speech and a very restricted exemption from arrest, these include: (1) the right of each house to regulate its own internal affairs and procedure; (2) the right to expel M.P.s and to determine qualifications to sit in either house; and (3) the right to secure the punishment of members and other persons for breach of privilege or contempt.

ROYAL ASSENT: bills passed by parliament are listed in a schedule attached to a commission under the great seal, naming three peers before whom the clerk of the parliaments pronounces the mediaeval formula, *La Reyne le veult* (with variations appropriate to money bills and private bills); without the royal assent they would not become law, but it has never been withheld since 1707.

ROYAL COMMISSION: advisory body appointed by royal warrant to investigate by questioning of expert witnesses, etc., a subject of major public importance, their report being eventually presented by the home secretary to the sovereign.

ROYAL PREROGATIVE: legally recognized powers of the crown other than those conferred by statute, which normally are exercised by the government of the day without prior recourse to parliament; they range from the control, organization, and disposition of all armed forces to the sole right of printing the Bible and book of common prayer.

RULE OF LAW: a constitutional principle, implying the supremacy of statute law and common law as administered in the ordinary law courts; this is contrasted with arbitrary governmental authority, superiority of status given to officials, and the derivation of private rights from a constitutional code; broadly speaking, the rule of law in this sense is specially characteristic of the British constitutional way of thinking.

SECRETARY OF STATE: an important office under the Tudors, and in the seventeenth and eighteenth centuries commonly divided into a northern and a southern department, of which the latter included home affairs; the third secretaryship became permanently established in 1794, and was subdivided into war and colonies in 1854; India was added in 1858, air, dominions, and Scotland in 1918–26; in legal theory any secretary can fulfil the duties of each secretaryship.

SELECT COMMITTEES: these include various sessional committees appointed by either house of parliament (e.g. commons committee of public accounts); committees of not more than 15 members may also be appointed to inquire into any matter of public concern and report to the house, for which purpose the house of commons usually gives power 'to send for persons, papers, and records'.

Notes and Definitions

SESSION OF PARLIAMENT: series of parliamentary sittings, usually about a year in length, terminated by a prorogation by the crown, which the lord chancellor announces together with the date of re-assembly; prorogation normally invalidates all progress made with bills that have not received the royal assent; parliament is always prorogued in advance of a proclamation of its dissolution and a general election.

SHERIFF: originally the chief representative of the crown in each county, now a landowner performing ceremonial functions, such as attendance on the judge at assizes; the clerk of the county council usually acts for him as returning officer at elections, the under-sheriff (a local solicitor) in the legal duties, such as summoning juries and taking responsibility for the execution of capital sentences.

SOVEREIGNTY OF PARLIAMENT: subject to the royal assent, parliament has a legally unrestricted power of legislation, since it can repeal any existing statute and override by express statement any hitherto accepted principle of common law; in practice as distinct from legal theory, legislation that outrages the feelings of the community would not be obeyed and is therefore beyond the effective competence of parliament.

SPEAKER: presiding officer elected by members of commons (since 1384 or earlier) at royal command to speak on their behalf in all parliamentary proceedings; now ranks as the sixth dignitary of the realm; his main function the control of debates, where his authority is virtually absolute. The powers of the lord chancellor as Speaker of the upper house are almost purely formal.

STATUTE OF WESTMINSTER: legislation passed by the United Kingdom parliament in 1931 to give effect to resolutions of the imperial conferences of 1926 and 1930; (a) dominions to be recognized as having full legislative powers, including the power to repeal United Kingdom legislation as affecting them; (b) dominions to be able to make laws having extra-territorial operation; (c) no future legislation of the United Kingdom parliament to extend to any dominion except at its express request.

STATUTORY INSTRUMENTS: the name used for all orders in council and departmental rules and regulations issued under legislative powers delegated to ministers by act of parliament; one reason for the tightening-up of parliamentary control by the statutory instruments act of 1946 was the discovery in 1944 that national fire service regulations had been enforced for three years without being laid before parliament as the law demanded.

SURCHARGE: a payment required from an office-holder on account of illegal expenditure; accounts of local government bodies, when examined by district auditors of the ministry of housing and local government, may be surcharged for making payments unauthorized by statute or making extravagant payments for authorized purposes; a surcharge over £500 disqualifies for continued membership of the authority.

ULTRA VIRES: a doctrine that justifies the law courts in restraining any authority except parliament from exceeding its lawful powers; it may be held that statutory powers have been exceeded, or that they have been used improperly or in defiance of principles of natural justice, or that a public authority has interfered unwarrantably with private rights which could have been defended against an individual.

VESTRIES: assemblies of parishioners, named from their place of meeting, which levied the church rate and appointed local officials; their powers were often usurped by select vestries, formed by co-option; elections, with additional votes for wealthier ratepayers, were instituted by statute in 1818; compulsory church rates were abolished in 1868, and vestries were eventually replaced by parish and parochial church councils.

BOOKS FOR FURTHER STUDY

GENERAL

D. L. KEIR: *Constitutional History of Modern Britain*, 6th edition, 1960
E. C. S. WADE and G. G. PHILLIPS: *Constitutional Law*, 6th edition, 1960
W. HARRISON: *The Government of Britain*, 6th edition, 1960
Sir William R. ANSON: *The Law and Custom of the Constitution*, Vol. I (edited by M. L. GWYER), 1922; Vols. II and III (edited by A. B. KEITH), 1935
K. C. WHEARE: *Government by Committee*, 1955
Sir Ivor JENNINGS: *The Law and the Constitution*, 4th edition, 1952
L. S. AMERY: *Thoughts on the Constitution*, 2nd edition, 1953
H. J. LASKI: *Reflections on the Constitution*, 1951
Lord CAMPION et al.: *British Government since 1918*, 1950
G. MARSHALL and G. C. MOODIE: *Some Problems of the Constitution*, 3rd edition, 1961

CHAPTER REFERENCES

I

W. BAGEHOT: *The English Constitution* (with introduction by Lord BALFOUR), 1928
A. V. DICEY: *Law of the Constitution* (with introduction by E. C. S. WADE), 1959
Sir M. AMOS: *The English Constitution*, 1930
Sir S. LOW: *The Governance of England*, revised edition, 1914

II

D. E. Butler: *The Electoral System in Britain, 1918–51*, 1953
D. E. Butler and R. Rose: *The British General Election of 1959*, 1960
R. T. McKenzie: *British Political Parties*, 1955
I. Bulmer Thomas: *The Party System in Great Britain*, 1953
Sir Ivor Jennings: *Party Politics*, 3 vols., 1960-2

III

N. Wilding and P. Laundy: *Encyclopaedia of Parliament*, 1958
E. Taylor: *The House of Commons at Work*, 3rd edition, 1957
Sir Ivor Jennings: *Parliament*, 2nd edition, 1957
Lord Campion et al.: *Parliament: A Survey*, 1952
Sir C. Ilbert: *Parliament* (revised by Sir C. Carr), 1948
A. P. Herbert: *The Point of Parliament*, 1946
P. A. Bromhead: *The House of Lords and Contemporary Politics 1911–1957*, 1958
D. N. Chester and N. Bowring: *Questions in Parliament*, 1962

IV

Sir Ivor Jennings: *Cabinet Government*, 3rd edition, 1959
Lord Morrison: *Government and Parliament*, 2nd edition, 1959
A. B. Keith: *The British Cabinet System* (edited by N. H. Gibbs), 1952

V

D. Morrah: *The Work of the Queen*, 1958
Sir Charles Petrie: *The Modern British Monarchy*, 1961
A. B. Keith: *The King and the Imperial Crown*, 1936

VI

R. M. Jackson: *The Machinery of Justice in England*, 3rd edition, 1960

H. G. HANBURY: *The English Courts of Law*, 3rd edition, 1960

VII

J. J. CLARKE: *Outlines of Central Government*, 13th edition, 1961

W. J. M. MACKENZIE and J. W. GROVE: *Central Administration in Britain*, 1957

F. M. G. WILLSON: *Organization of British Central Government 1914–56* (edited by D. N. CHESTER), 1957

F. DUNNILL: *The Civil Service—Some Human Aspects*, 1956

Lord STRANG: *The Foreign Office*, 1955

Sir F. NEWSAM: *The Home Office*, 2nd edition, 1955

F. A. JOHNSON: *Defence by Committee: The British Committee of Imperial Defence, 1885–1959*, 1960

VIII & X

M. P. HALL: *The Social Services of Modern England*, 5th edition, 1960

NATIONAL COUNCIL OF SOCIAL SERVICE: *Public Social Services*, 10th edition, 1955

A. H. HAYNES: *Practitioners' Handbook to the Social Services*, 1955

P. ARCHER (editor): *Social Welfare and the Citizen*, 1957

B. N. RODGERS and J. DIXON: *Portrait of Social Work*, 1960

M. BRUCE: *The Coming of the Welfare State*, 1961

IX

W. E. JACKSON: *Structure of Local Government in England and Wales*, 4th edition, 1960

J. J. CLARKE: *Outlines of the Local Government of the United Kingdom*, 19th edition, 1960

Sir J. MAUD and S. E. FINER: *Local Government in England and Wales*, 2nd edition, 1953

J. H. WARREN: *The English Local Government System*, 3rd edition, 1953

K. B. SMELLIE: *History of Local Government*, 3rd edition, 1957

XI
Lord MORRISON: *How London Is Governed*, revised edition, 1948
M. COLE: *Servant of the County*, 1956

XII
V. BRITTAIN: *Lady into Woman*, 1953

XIII
E. L. WIGHAM: *Trade Unions*, 1956
Lady (Mary) MORRIS: *Voluntary Organizations and Social Progress*, 1955
H. A. MESS (editor): *Voluntary Social Services since 1918*, 1947

XIV
K. C. WHEARE: *The Constitutional Structure of the Commonwealth*, 1960
CENTRAL OFFICE OF INFORMATION: *The Commonwealth in Brief*, 1960
Sir C. JEFFRIES: *The Colonial Office*, 1956

XV
POLITICAL AND ECONOMIC PLANNING: *European Organizations*, 1959
TREASURY INFORMATION DIVISION AND C. O. I.: *Britain and the European Communities*, 1962
G. L. GOODWIN: *Britain and the United Nations*, 1957
U. N. OFFICE OF PUBLIC INFORMATION: *Everyman's United Nations*, 6th edition, 1960

INDEX

A King's Story, 66
Accession ceremonies, 4, 52, 68
Administrative law, 97–9, 228
Adoptive acts, 140, 224
Advisory council on tribunals, 99
Africa: Commonwealth states of, 193, 194, 199, 201, 218; *see also* High commission territories, South Africa, South-West Africa
Air Force, Royal, 60, 100–2, 104–5, 196
Albert, Prince (1819–61), 66
Aldermen, 137, 138, 159, 160–1
Ambassadors, *see* Diplomatic representation
Anne (reigned 1702–14), 49–50, 224
ANZUS treaty, 190
Appeal courts, 91–3
Appropriation bill, 37
Archbishops, 29, 33, 58, 60, 93, 172
Army, 60, 65, 100–4, 107, 186, 197, 202
Asquith, H. H. (1852–1928), 52, 166
Assistance Boards, 117, 119
Assizes, 6, 85, 86, 90, 91
Atomic energy authority, 125–6
Attlee, Lord, 71–2, 219
Attorney-general, 54, 89, 92, 227
Australasia, 75
Australia, 189, 190, 196, 198, 218

Bagehot, W. (1826–77), 1, 71
Bailie, 12

Baldwin, S. (1867–1947), 194
Balfour, Lord (1848–1930), 68, 106, 187
Balfour declaration, 76
Bank of England, 37, 114, 127, 226
BBC, 112, 126–7, 198
Bentham, J. (1748–1832), 88
Bevan, A. (1898–1960), 120, 156
Beveridge, Lord, 118
Bevin, E. (1884–1951), 72, 212
Bill of Rights, 67, 224, 228
Bishops, 29, 33, 60, 70, 172, 225
Blackstone, Sir W. (1723–80), 31, 225
Blake, R. (1599–1657), 101
BOAC, 127
Board of guardians, 133, 134, 165
Boroughs: history, 132–4; status, 82, 136; organization, 137: *see also* County borough
Brewster sessions, 138
British North America act, 189, 224
British Restaurants, 146
British subject, *see* Citizenship
Broadcasting, 69, 79; *see also* BBC
Brougham, Lord (1778–1868), 88
Budget, 37–41, 111
Burgh, 12
Burke, E. (1729–97), 26
By-elections, 23
By-laws, 141, 153, 225

237

Cabinet: history, 49–52; functions, 53–7, 59; *see also* Ministries
Cabinet committees, 57, 102
Cabinet conclusions, 59
Cabinet office (secretariat), 51, 59
Cambridge, Duke of (1819–1904), 65
Canada, 75, 94, 188, 189, 190, 196, 208, 209, 213, 224, 226
Canning, G. (1770–1827), 50
Capital punishment, 45, 91, 92, 231
Catholic Directory, 176
Central criminal court, 91, 161
Central electricity board, 127
Central electricity generating board, 129
Ceylon, 193
Chairman of (local) council, 138, 142, 159
Chamberlain, A. N. (1869–1940), 48
Chancellor, *see* Lord Chancellor
Chancellor of the Exchequer, 37, 54, 111
Chancery, 88, 93
Channel Isles, 15
Charity Organization Society, 180
Charles I (reigned 1625–49), 75, 87
Charles II (reigned 1660–85), 87, 100
Chiefs of Staff, 102, 197
Child welfare, 89, 110, 117, 119, 120, 123, 169, 173, 176, 179, 181, 182
Church assembly, 174
Church of England, 13, 60, 93, 167, 172–5
Church of Scotland, 12, 175
Churchill, Sir W., 48, 61, 71, 74, 75, 207, 208

Citizenship, 82, 188–9, 191
City, 136, 225
City of London, 157, 158, 160–1, 163
Civil list, 38, 225
Civil Service: history, 100, 107, 123–4; classes, 107–8; legal position, 83, 108–9; control by prime minister, 59, 60; functions, 55, 106–7, 109–14, 120; scientific branches, 123–6; regional organization, 108, 155
Clerk of the parliaments, 29, 229
Clerk of the peace, 90
Clerk, Town (or of other local government bodies), 142, 231
Closure, 32
Coal Board, 128–9
Coke, Sir E. (1552–1634), 225
Colombo plan, 196
Colonial development and welfare acts, 202
Colonial development corporation, 203
Colonial office, 79, 191, 202
Colonies, forms of government in, 199–201
Committee of imperial defence, 51, 52
Committee of public accounts, 37
Committee of supply, 36
Committee of the whole house, 36, 41
Committee of ways and means, 36–7
Common council, Court of, 161
Common law, 12, 86, 88, 101, 225, 227, 231
Common Market, 213–14
Commons, House of, 27–33, 35–48, 54, 56, 60, 62, 168
Commonwealth: relation to British crown, 77–80; development, 188–92, 215; increase

Index

in member states, 192-4; links and common institutions, 94, 195-7, 208, 216; centrifugal tendencies, 7, 191, 198, 214
Commonwealth Day, 66
Commonwealth Declaration, 192
Commonwealth prime ministers, Meetings of, 195
Commonwealth relations office, 191, 195, 199
Comprehensive schools, 150-1
Comptroller and auditor general, 37, 225
Condominium, 191, 199
Congé d'élire, 174
Consolidated fund, 37, 38, 114, 225, 226
Constable, 132; special, 228, 229
Constitution, Characteristics of British, 9-11
Conventions of the constitution, 92, 226
Convocation, 174
Co-operative societies, 179
Coram, T. (1668-1751), 179
Coronation, 5
Coroner, 95, 226
Council, Lord President of the, 53, 54, 124-5
Council of Europe, 211
Councillors of state, 82
County boroughs, 134-6
County colleges, 151, 152
County councils, 134, 137-8
County courts: medieval, 86, 131; modern, 92
Court of session, 12
Cripps, Sir Stafford (1889-1952), 192
Cromwell, Oliver (1599-1658), 30, 100
Crown, Powers of the, 80-3, 108-9
Crown court, 90

Cumberland, Duke of (1721-65), 65
Curragh mutiny, 102
Customs, 39, 40, 113

Dalton, Lord, 72
Darling, C. J. (1849-1936), 97
Declaration of rights, 224
Defence committee (of cabinet), 102
Defence minister, 102
Defence policy, 103-5, 196-7, 202, 210-11
Dependencies, 198-203, 218
Deputy prime minister, 74
Development corporations, 163-4
Diarchy, 186
Diplomatic representation, 70, 78, 110, 187; see also High Commissioners
Disraeli, B. (1804-81), 51, 153, 165
Dissolution of parliament, 21, 72-3, 231
Divisional Executive, 148
Dr. Barnardo's Homes, 179
Dominions, Status of, 76-7, 184-90, 191, 224
Drake, Sir F. (1545-96), 101
DSIR, 124-5
Durham, Lord (1792-1840), 226
Durham report, 75, 226

Economist, The, 1
Eden, Sir A. (Lord Avon), 75
Edinburgh, Duke of, 68
Education, 13, 116, 117, 148-52
Education, Ministry of, 149
Edward I (reigned 1272-1307), 5, 29, 172
Edward VI (reigned 1547-53), 29
Edward VII (reigned 1901-10), 66

Index

Edward VIII (reigned 1936), 66, 67, 77
Eire, *see* Ireland
Elections, Procedure in parliamentary, 19–23
Electricity council, 129
Eleven-plus examination, 150
Elgin, Lord (1807–63), 226
Elizabeth I (reigned 1558–1603), 30, 116, 133
Elizabeth II, 69–75, 77, 79–80
Elizabeth (queen consort 1936–52), 68
English Constitution, The, 1, 68, 71
Equity, 85, 88
Establishment, Church, 173
Estate duty, 114
Estimates (Parliamentary), 36–9
European economic community, *see* Common market
European free trade association, 214
Evening institutes, 151
Excepted Districts, 148
Excise, 39, 40, 113

Family allowances, 119, 168
Federations, 186–7, 189, 193, 194, 208, 213
Finances, National, 35–41
Fire service, 110, 158, 232
Foreign office, 54, 72, 109–10, 112; *see also* Diplomatic representation
Forestry commission, 112
Franchise: parliamentary, 16–19; local government, 132–4, 137, 160–1; extension to women, 166–7
Free church federal council, 175
Free churches, 13, 173, 175, 176
Free speech, 10
Freedom of the press, 10
Friendly societies, 179

Garden cities, 153
Gas council, 129
General assembly (Church of Scotland), 175
General strike, 177
George II (reigned 1727–60), 58, 65
George III (reigned 1760–1820), 50, 64–5, 75, 77
George IV (reigned 1820–30), 50, 65, 88
George V (reigned 1910–36), 67, 80, 82, 228
George VI (reigned 1936–52), 67, 71–2, 77, 192
Gladstone, W. E. (1809–98), 51, 52, 66, 115
Governor, 79, 200
Governor-general, 76–7, 79, 80, 188, 195
Grand jury, 86
Grants-in-aid, 146–7
Green Belt, 160
Grenville, Lord (1759–1834), 65
Guillotine (closure), 32
Guy, T. (1645–1724), 179

Habeas Corpus, 97, 103, 227
Haldane, Lord (1856–1928), 124
Head of civil service, 111
Head of the Commonwealth, 78, 188
Health, Ministry of, 120–3
Health service, 120–3, 179
Henry II (reigned 1154–89), 84, 86
Henry VIII (reigned 1509–47), 11
Heralds, College of, 4
High commission territories, 199, 76
High commissioners, 195
High court of justice, 91–3
Hill, O. (1838–1912), 180

Index

Hogarth, W. (1697-1764), 6
Home office, 15, 110-11, 112
Home rule act, 102, 228
Hong Kong, 190, 199
Honours list, 69
Hospitals, 121-2, 179
Housing, 119, 152-6, 159-60
Housing and local government, Ministry of, 98, 140, 146, 155, 163, 232
Howard, E. (1850-1928), 153
Howard, J. (1726-90), 179
Human rights, Convention for protection of, 211, 220
Hustings, 19

Imperial conferences, 76, 187, 191
Imperial defence college, 197
Imperial war cabinet, 185
Income tax, 39, 114
India, 76, 78, 184, 185-7, 190, 191-3
Indirect rule, 201
Inland revenue, Board of, 114, 144
Inns of court, 87
Insurance, *see* Social insurance
International court of justice, 206, 216
Ireland (*see also* Northern Ireland), 14, 34, 77-8, 102-3, 185, 188, 189, 190, 191
Isle of Man, 15

James I (reigned 1603-25), 11, 19
James II (reigned 1685-8), 4
Joint services staff college, 197
Jubilees, Royal, 68, 76
Judges: how appointed, 55, 84-5, 87; how organized, 91-4
Judicature act, 87-8
Judicial Committee of Privy Council, 52, 94, 189, 202

Jury system, 12, 86-7, 90-3, 95, 231
Justices of the peace, 87, 89-90, 131, 134, 138, 169, 227
Juvenile court, 89, 169

Kaisar-i-Hind, 76
Kangaroo (procedure), 32
Kipling, R. (1865-1936), 76
Kitchener, Lord (1850-1916), 101

Lambeth conferences, 175
Laud, Archbishop W. (1573-1645), 75
Leader of the house of commons, 60
Leader of the Opposition, 61, 74
League of nations, 184, 185, 205-7
League of nations union, 171
Legal aid, 96
Legitimist Calendar, 224
Libraries, 152, 224
Life Peerages, 34, 92
Livery companies, 160
Lloyd George, D. (1863-1945), 51, 117, 125, 126, 185
Local education authority, 148
Local government: history, 131-5; organization, 12, 135-43; finances, 144-8; provision of education and housing, 148-56; in London, 135, 157-64; royal commissions, 134-5
London county council, 158-60, 162-3, 169
London (Passenger) Transport Board, 162
London season, 35, 70
Lord Chancellor, 30, 38, 54-5, 58, 85, 92, 98, 99, 227
Lord chief justice, 91
Lord lieutenant, 138

Lords, House of, 29–35, 42, 44, 55, 72, 75, 168, 173; judicial functions, 92–3
Lords of appeal in ordinary, 34, 92, 94
Lugard, Lord (1858–1945), 101, 201

Macmillan, H., 75, 193
Magistrates' court, 89
Magna Carta, 85, 227
Malaya, 78, 190, 193
Mandamus writ, 98, 140, 227
Mandates, 184, 199, 218
Manor court, 86, 132
Markets, 132, 146, 161
Marshall plan, 212
Martial law, 102–3, 227
Mary II (reigned 1689–94), 4, 64, 224
Mary (queen consort 1910–36), 67, 80
Mayor, 6, 21, 137, 141, 142, 160, 162, 169
Members of parliament: qualifications, 24; functions, 26–8, 41–8; privileges, 30, 229
Metropolitan institutions: board of works, 158; boroughs, 158, 160; magistrates, 90; police, 161–2, 170; *see also* London, City of London
Mill, J. S. (1806–73), 165
Ministers of state, 54
Ministries, formation and termination of, 47–8; composition, 53–4; *see also* Cabinet
Monarchy: history, 49–50, 64–8; U.K. functions, 5, 58, 68–75; Commonwealth functions, 75–80; *see also* Crown
Montesquieu, C. L. de S. de (1689–1755), 8
Morley, J. (1838–1923), 51

Municipal corporations act, 133, 160
Municipal trading, 145–6
Mutiny act, 101

National Children's Home, 179
National Council of Social Service, 182–3
National Council of Women, 171
National debt, 38, 40, 115
National service, 101, 104
NATO, 209–11, 217
Natural justice, 99, 228, 232
Nature Conservancy, 125
Navy, Royal, 60, 100–2, 104, 188, 190
Newspapers, influence of, 10, 23, 28, 48, 79, 173, 198
New towns, 155, 163
New Zealand, 189, 190, 196, 198, 218
Nightingale, F. (1820–1910), 165
Nonconformists, *see* Free churches
Northern Ireland, 14, 102, 173
Nursery schools, 149

OECD, OEEC, 212–13, 217
Old age pensions, 2, 116–17
Old Bailey, *see* Central criminal court
Old people, Care of, 2, 116, 119, 123, 148, 176, 182
Opposition, Parliamentary, 61–3, 74
Orders in council, 52, 81, 98, 107, 228, 232
Ordnance survey, 112
Ottawa conference, 189–90
Overseers of the poor, 132

Pakistan, 78, 193
Palmerston, Lord (1784–1865), 31, 66

Index

Pankhurst, E. (1858–1928), 166
Parish organization, 132, 139, 174, 232
Parliament acts, 33, 42, 228
Parliament, history of, 29–35; see also Commons and Lords, Houses of
Parliamentary reform, 16–18, 226–7
Parties, Political, 24–8, 56, 59, 62–3, 74, 106, 108, 141, 159, 177
Peel, Sir R. (1788–1850), 51, 161–2
Peers, Creation of, 29, 30, 34, 72, 228
Permanent secretary, under-secretary, 109
Petition of Right, 83, 102, 228
Petitioning, 228
Petty sessions, see Magistrates' court
Pitt, W. (1708–78), 61
Pitt, W. (1759–1806), 34, 65, 226
Placemen, 53
Police, 88–9, 138, 147, 161–2, 169–70, 229; see also Constable
Poor law, 116, 119, 121, 133
Port of London Authority, 112, 162
Post office, 83, 109, 112, 128
Prerogative powers, 81–3, 228, 230
Prime minister, 34, 50, 51, 53–61, 69, 71–5, 174, 193
Private bills, 43–4, 133, 229
Private members' bills, 42–3
Privy Council, 4, 30, 49, 51, 52, 56; see also Judicial Committee
Protected states, 199
Protectorates, 184, 185, 199
Provost, 12
Public bill procedure, 41–5

Public schools, 149
Public utilities, 112, 126

Quakers, 176
Quarter sessions, 90
Queen's Bench Division, 91, 93, 227
Queen's Speech, 5, 46–7
Questions in parliament, 28, 45–6

Ragged schools, 179
Raikes, R. (1735–1811), 179
Ralegh, Sir W. (1552–1618), 101
Rates, 144–6, 148, 156
Recorder, 90, 161, 169
Regency, Provisions for, 67–8, 77, 82
Report on Social Insurance and the Allied Services, 118
Republics, 78, 191–2, 193, 195
Reserving of bills, 75
Reuters, 197
Revolution of 1688, 4, 31
Rhodes, C. J. (1853–1902), 101
Roman Catholic church, 173, 176
Roman law, 12, 86, 87
Rome, Treaty of, 214
Royal assent, 42, 226
Royal commission, 134, 229
Rule of Law, 9, 230
Rural district councils, 134, 139

Salisbury, 3rd Marquess (1830–1903), 158; 5th Marquess, 75
Salvation Army, 176
School boards, 133, 134
Scotland, 11–13, 18, 34, 54, 99, 173, 175
SEATO, 219
Secretaries of state, 53, 55, 230; see also Colonial office, etc.
Select committees, 97, 230
Self-help, 180
Session of parliament, 231

Settlement, Act of, 67, **224**
Sex disqualification (removal) act, 167
Shaftesbury, Lord (1801–85), 179
Sheriff, 5–6, 21, 160, 228, 231
Slum clearance, 153–5, 159
Smiles, S. (1812–1904), 180
Social assistance, 116–20
Social insurance, 2, 116–20
Social service (voluntary), 179–83
Solicitor-general, 54
Sophia, Princess (1630–1714), 67, 224
South Africa, 75, 76, 77, 94, 188, 190, 194, 195, 198, 199
South-West Africa, 184, 199
Sovereignty of parliament, 11, 231
Speaker, 29, 32, 33, 38, 44, 46, 98, 231
Special areas, 118
Special jury, 93
Standing committees (parliamentary), 41
Standing joint committees, 138, 160
State opening of parliament, 5
Statutory authorities, 133, 157
Statutory instruments, 98, 232
Sterling area, 196
Stipendiary magistrates, 90
Suez canal, 103, 185
Sunday schools, 173, 179
Supply days, 36
Surcharge, 147, 232
Surtax, 39, 114

Taxation, 37, 113–15
Television, 5, 23, 69, 79, 173
Ten-minute rule, 42
Thames conservancy, 162
Times, The, 10
Toleration act, 173

Tone, W. (1763–98), 103
Town (and country) planning, 153–6
Trades union congress, 167, 177, 212
Trade unions, 176–8
Transport, Ministry of, 127–8
Transport nationalization, 128–30
Treasury, 111–12, 115, 155; first lord of, 53; junior lords, 54
Treasury counsel, 57
Trust territories, 199, 218
Tynwald, 15

Ulster, *see* Northern Ireland
Ultra Vires doctrine, 140, 225, 232
UNESCO, 219
United Kingdom, 11–14
United Nations, 215–20
United nations association, 215
Universities, 13, 19, 60, 82, 149, 151–2, 159, 166, 197
University extension movement, 151
University grants committee, 151
University settlements, 180
Urban district councils, 134, 136, 138, 139

Vestries, 132, 157, 158, 232
Victoria (reigned 1837–1901), 51, 65–6, 72, 75, 76, 81, 173, 184, 191, 192
Vote of credit, 38

Wales, 11, 13, 18, 173, 228
Walpole, Sir R. (1676–1745), 50, 51, 52, 58
War cabinet, 51
Wards, 137
Watch committee, 138
Water supply, 139, 145, 153, 162

Index

Welfare state, 1–3, 62, 99, 123, 220
Wentworth, Sir T. (1593–1641), 75
West Indies, Federation of the, 194, 200
Western European Union, 209
Westminster, Statute of, 187, 189, 231
Whips, 45, 54
William I (reigned 1066–87), 5, 84, 100
William III (reigned 1689–1702), 4, 49, 64, 224
William IV (reigned 1830–7), 50, 65
Witenagemot, 4
Women: franchise, 165–7; control of property, 166; admission to public office, 166–8; disabilities, 167; employment, 167, 169–70; social service, 168, 170–1
Women's Institutes, 170
Women's Voluntary Services, 171, 181
Workers' educational association, 151
Works, Ministry of, 112

York, Duke of (1763–1827), 65
Youth clubs, 152, 182

Date D